Adam Lyal's

Witchery Tales

The darker side of Old Edinburgh

Illustrations by
Alan McGowan

Published for

THE CADIES

by Moubray House Press

EDINBURGH 1988

Adam Lyal (deceased) would like to acknowledge the help and support of the following souls:

Mr James Thomson of Castlehill
Mr Rollo Mitchell of Scoonie
Ms Vivien Robertson of Knockanharrie
Ms Cathleen Tulloch of Househill
Mr Nic Allen of Snook

For further information on our ghostly excursions, books and Scottish video productions, including "Adam Lyal's Royal Mile", "Georgian Edinburgh", "St. Andrews" and "The Ghosts of Scotland"

Contact:
The Cadies/Witchery Tours
352 Castlehill
Royal Mile
Edinburgh
EH1 2NF
Tel: 0131 225 6745
Fax: 0131 220 2086
email: lyal@witcherytours.demon.co.uk
http://www.witcherytours.com
http://www.scotweb.co.uk/underthekilt/

ISBN 0948473088

Typeset by Anagram Word Services, Edinburgh
Printed and bound by The Bath Press, Bath

Contents

Foreword

Just under a century ago Robert Louis Stevenson wrote of the legends of his native city as a body of tradition which by survival of the fittest had become a work of art. Those who have had the good fortune to follow the authors in their guises of Adam Lyal and his ghostly companions, in a pilgrimage through what remain of the tall lands and arched passageways of the Old Town, will, in reading this book, readily conjure up Stevenson's picture of the low dens and high-flying garrets where "people may go back upon the dark passages in the town's adventures" and like them "chill their marrow with winter's tales about the fire". Other less fortunate visitors will find in this book true tales stranger than fiction, tales singularly apposite and characteristic of old Edinburgh life. They may perhaps enhance the horror of the tales by imagining them told as the wind pipes and hoots round the buildings and down the spine of the Old Town from the Castle to Holyrood.

The authors in their chosen calling as modern day Cadies guiding others through the closes of the Old Town, have acted upon the adage that every stone tells a tale. Their message deserved a wider audience. In this little book they present it too on a larger stage in a fascinating fashion fit to satisfy the curiosity—morbid or otherwise—of anyone who, becoming acquainted with Edinburgh, seeks to find the romance behind the stiff, grey facade of its buildings.

Cameron of Lochbroom

Introduction

Welcome to "Adam Lyal's Witchery Tales", a volume which although slim, is an able and meritous production. But more of this presently, first of all I must introduce myself. I am known as Adam Lyal (Deceased) and must confess to having been at one time a ne'er-do-well of the Old Town of Edinburgh.

Should you wish to search me out my name is still in the records, unfortunately on the list of executions. My life of crime came to a sad end on the hangman's scaffold as I was executed on the 27th March 1811 for the small matter of highway robbery.

If the citizens of Edinburgh thought they had seen the last of me they were wrong. I have returned of late to this mortal world and can again be seen moving stealthily through the Old Town shadows. My return is no accident, no quirk of time or of nature. I was summoned from my penance by the "Man in Black", the owner of The Witchery by the Castle. He called upon me for my knowledge of the darker side of Edinburgh's history, to act as a guide for some mortal fellows who he wished not only to enjoy Edinburgh's most haunted restaurant but also to remain spellbound afterwards on a walk through the murky alleyways and secluded courtyards of this ancient city.

It was on Halloween's night 1985 that I first re-appeared outside the Witchery restaurant on the Castlehill. The building that had lain semi-derelict for more than 120 years seemed to be filled with new life, there was eating, drinking, much laughter and merriment. The tour was a great success and I so enjoyed telling my tales that when the "Man in Black" began to summon me on a more regular basis I was delighted, and so the "Witchery Murder and Mystery Tour" was born. As time progressed psychic forces must have spread word of my endeavours beyond the walls of the Witchery, for now groups of locals and visitors from all walks of life will call upon me when they feel the desire to step back through the centuries. Under the cloak of darkness, information and imagination are a heady potion which can bring past events and lives seeping through the mortar and stone of the Old Town walls.

Over the years the questions and demands for more information have been many and I have endeavoured in this volume to merit the liberal encouragement received in the past. It is a good collection of convenient size and inside you will find many authentic tales from Edinburgh's long and gory history. There are, for instance, dark accounts of violence and crime, vivid descriptions of hangings and executions, information on plagues and disasters, and finally haunting tales of witchcraft and the supernatural.

Whether you are a local or a visitor I hope this book will bring you something of the character and atmosphere of the Old Town and that the stories will kindle an interest in the wealth of fascinating history connected with our dear "Auld Reekie". Search further and you will always be richly rewarded.

Having met many of the characters mentioned within I am confident that you will enjoy this book and finally I would beg leave to suggest you read on and enjoy "Adam Lyal's Witchery Tales".

Adam Lyal (Deceased)
March 1988

Chapter One

Rough Justice

As you can imagine I have first hand experience of 'rough justice' so it would be my pleasure to take you from corporal punishment to death by beheading. A grisly tour of the great variety of sentences imposed on those of us unfortunate enough to get caught.

One of the mildest forms of punishment was fines. These were not physically painful, but could be financially crippling. In 1648 Andrew Brand, a merchant, had his burgess ticket cancelled for insulting a bailie. This meant he could no longer do business — a situation which lasted for two years. Fines or confiscation of property was applied in many minor cases.

Banishment from the city was quite common, it was often used to rid the streets of hordes of travelling beggars. But it could also mean transportation to the American Colonies or, after 1788, to somewhere like Botany Bay in Australia. For example, in June 1654 16 rebel soldiers were taken from the Canongate Tolbooth and shipped to Barbados to be sold as slaves. About ten years later due to a shortage of labour the privy council granted that 'vagabonds' and criminals could also be transported to the plantations in Barbados. It is ironic that nowadays criminals can't wait to earn enough to transport themselves to places in the sun!

It is easy to forget how popular corporal punishments were in the old days, especially in the early centuries of the burgh. Imagine if you were caught for some minor offence nowadays and could face being sentenced to the stocks or the pillory. Perhaps if your crime was a little more serious you might have your tongue pierced, be publicly whipped, burned on the cheek or have an ear, hand or foot amputated. It was no consolation that these punishments were not all carried out at once.

If you had to choose one of these perhaps it would be whipping or 'scourging' as it was also called. These took place at 9 whipping sites around the city. One of these places was called Stripping Close, an alleyway situated on the Castlehill where the Tolbooth St John's church now stands. It was here on July 31st 1822 that 3 men were publicly whipped for assault. This was the last time that the citizens of Edinburgh were to witness this harsh punishment being inflicted. One sure way of attracting a lot of attention was to be whipped on the move! A typical example comes from the Tolbooth records of 1657 (translation from Scots):

> 'November 7th — Agnes Anderson as found guilty of adultery with Pet Ealing in Kirkliston was ordained by the honourable commissioners upon Wednesday next the 12th of this instant between 11 and 12 hours before noon to be whipped from the Castlehill to the Netherbow (about half a mile) and thereafter to be set at liberty'.

It is interesting to note that on the same day William Miller was whipped 'privately' in the Tolbooth. Did a 'brybe' save him from public humiliation?

Drowning was a mode of execution considered a little more delicate than hanging and the considerate (male) judges of the day tended to reserve it for women. For example, in October 1530 the death sentence was passed on two women who had broken some of the strict laws enforced to prevent the spread of the plague. It was for these crimes that the women were taken out to the Greyfriars Port Quarry Hole and drowned.

Hanging was the most common form of death penalty and the

gallows were efficient and easy to operate. The criminals soon got the hang of it. I would like to have described to you my own demise, but it would bring back too many horrible memories. However, a few interesting hangings do spring to mind!

In some cases crimes that led people to the scaffold seem very minor by today's standards. In May 1770 William Harris was publicly executed for forgery. Thomas Urquhart (postmaster) and George Warden were both hanged for opening letters that didn't belong to them.

An unusual case features in *Book IV of the Old Edinburgh Club*. The account describes a person who was hanged for 'irregularities of conduct'. This may be connected to the fact that Margaret Rannie was 'both man and woman, a thing not ordinary in this Kingdom'. After death he/she was opened up by doctors who were surprised to find the corpse to be 'two every way, having two hearts, two livers, two of every inward thing'. Unfortunately for Margaret Rannie, the one rope was singularly efficient.

The Execution of Mary MacKinnon — An Eyewitness Account

The eye-witness information for this next account comes from pamphlets printed and sold at the Edinburgh Observer office in Mound Place. These biographical accounts, which usually ended with a description of the criminal's conduct at trial, were very popular. They were also used to make moral comment and warn others of similar behaviour. The pamphlets had something to say about the drunken state of those who were involved in a fracas that led to murder. 'Spiritous liquors respect not persons', rather they 'leighten the folly of the foolish and deprive the rational of reason'.

The pamphlets also described how Mary MacKinnon was sentenced to be executed on the 16th of April 1823 for the murder of a young clerk called William Howat. His death came as a result of a drunken squabble in a disreputable Edinburgh tavern.

After being found guilty, Mary MacKinnon was sent to Calton Jail where she 'entertained confident expectations of receiving the Royal mercy'. This was not to be.

It was 6 o'clock on a Wednesday morning that she awoke to face the 'black trap-stair that leads to the scaffold'. At 7am she 'engaged in services of religion' and at 8 she said she was ready to depart for the Grassmarket where her execution was to take place.

It was described at the time in this way:

'The unfortunate woman was plainly and genteelly dressed, she wore a black silk gown, coloured shawl, black straw bonnet and black veil.

Assembled to witness the melancholy spectacle were a crowd that cannot be estimated at less than 20,000. The windows and roof tops were crowded, every corner eagerly seized. But there was no tumult or disorder, the utmost peace and quiet prevailed throughout the whole scene.

About 20 minutes past eight she ascended the fatal steps. After the prisoner had been seated a very impressive prayer was delivered by Mr Thomson. She listened with indifference and actually fainted at the close of it — a draught of water revived her.

She called the bailies and the clergy-man and made a solemn disavowal of the murder. Having disburdened her mind she sat down on the drop, a deadly paleness on her countenance.

Then an orange was handed to her, and while she was eating it, she conversed coolly with the surgeon. A linen cap was then drawn over her features. After the rope was adjusted she withdrew the cap and waved goodbye to the crowd. She shook hands with those around her, re-adjusted the cap and the fatal signal was given. In a few minutes all was over. Her struggles were short, there were only two convulsions of nature.'

The pamphlets then end with this final justification. 'If a most severe example be not made when crimes are committed, the consequences may be easily imagined — we can pity the woman, but cannot forgive the crime'.

Mary MacKinnon's hanging was well organised and successfully carried out. Unfortunately, there has been more than one occasion where things have not gone so well. At the hanging of Philip Stanfield in 1688 it is reported that the executioner had to step in and finish the job himself, with his bare hands.

The execution of Robert Johnson, December 30th 1818

'I have just returned from being an involuntary witness to one of the most horrible scenes which ever disgraced the execution of public justice'.

So wrote an eye-witness to the hanging of Robert Johnston on a cold December afternoon outside the church of St Giles in the year 1818. Robert Johnston's crimes were of little consequence; he had been sentenced to death for robbery and wouldn't have been remembered had it not been for the great outrage following the incompetent handling of his execution.

Reading this letter of complaint to the magistrates, you can imagine the scene. The condemned man is 'shivering on the brink of eternity'. The psalm singing is over and the magistrates stand around the scaffold in their red gowns as the new hangman fixes the rope round Johnston's neck. An expectant hush falls across the crowd and many turn their backs in that final moment as the thief is jerked into the air; his body swings across to suspend above the platform.

Suddenly, there is a shout of 'Good God, the man's feet are not off the scaffold'. Those who could not bear to watch turn round and see that Johnston's feet can just touch the platform because the new hangman has made the rope too long. The compression of the rope on his windpipe is not enough to steal his life, but sufficient to cause excruciating pain. He still seems to be in command of his senses because 3 times he bends his legs upwards, apparently in a desperate attempt to hasten an end to his agony.

The magistrates stand passive and the crowd begin to grow restless. Shortly, carpenters arrive and spend ten minutes trying to cut the wood away from underneath the suffering criminal. This makes no difference and the crowd, now angry, begin to throw stones at the authorities around the scaffold. The magistrates and hangman retreat to the safety of the Tolbooth Church followed by the derision of the crowd. The magistrates were later criticised for their lack of action and for deserting their posts.

Meanwhile, a member of the crowd has climbed up and cut Johnston down and he now lies 'panting on the scaffold'. He's been released from his agony, but not from his sentence. The crowd's sympathy for his suffering does not stretch as far as to allow him to escape. In fact, there are many cries of 'No rescue!'

Johnston is then helped to the police office, still gasping after his awful ordeal. The crowd gathers outside but the doors are shut and bolted. Some of the crowd start to disperse as they presume this was the end of the spectacle. Unfortunately Johnston, having recovered, is taken back to the adjusted gallows and, alas, hanged for the second time... successfully.

Cheating Death in a Graveyard

On the 24th of November 1783 an advertisement appeared in the Edinburgh Advertiser:

> 'John Hay, indicted for highway robbery, aged about 18 years, by trade a glazier, 5 feet 10 inches high, slender made, pale complexion, long visage, brown hair cut short, pitted a little in the face with the small pox, speaks slow with a haar in his tone, and has a mole on one of his cheeks. The magistrates offer a reward of twenty guineas to any person who will apprehend and secure the said John Hay being recommitted to the Tolbooth of this city'.

Two things are remarkable about Hay. The first is that he managed to escape from the Edinburgh Tolbooth and the second is that he remained undetected in the city for 6 weeks.

But one thing at a time. A few days before the date set for his execution Hay's father came to visit, bringing with him some strong liquor. The jailer decided it would be impolite to refuse the kind offer of a drink and a few hours later he could hardly move.

Hay and his father proceeded to the outer door where Hay's father called out 'turn your hand'. These were the words used when a jailer wanted to leave the building. The door opened only a fraction, but as young Hay was 'slender made' he managed to dart out into the night air. Once into the warren of closes he was gone.

His place of survival for 6 weeks was the mausoleum of Sir George MacKenzie in the Greyfriars Kirkyard. He was fed by the boys of the adjacent Heriots School. They decided to help because James Hay was an ex 'Herioter'. After this he escaped abroad, saved by an old boy network that went as far as the grave, in this case Sir George MacKenzie's.

Half-Hangit Maggie Dickson

An unusual but very appropriate nickname for a lady who was convicted of murder. Maggie Dickson was tried under the Concealment of Pregnancy Act of 1690. She had had a premature baby and when it died she tried to hide the body.

The jury found her guilty of child murder and on the 2nd of September 1724 she was hanged. She was to be buried in her home town of Musselburgh. A horse and cart set out from Edinburgh carrying the coffin. About half way to her final resting place Maggie Dickson recovered. This news was of course considered quite incredible and it spread like wildfire. She was the talk of the town and her escape from the brink of death promoted a great debate. The question of the moment was whether or not she should be re-hanged.

In the end, after much discussion and various theories put forward as to why she survived, it was decided she should be allowed to go free. After all, the magistrates had pronounced her dead.

She was to live a further 30 years in which time no-one ever discovered how it was she had survived her own hanging. But it was enough time for her to be given the most famous nickname of the day — 'Half-Hangit Maggie', because she was only half hung!

The last woman to be hanged in Edinburgh was Jessie King. She was tried on the 18th of February 1889 for the murder of 3 small children. She had taken sums of money from parents to cover the costs of the supposed 'adoptions'.

The Lord Justice Clerk found her guilty and told her 'You shall be hanged on the 11th day of March, between the hours of 8 and 10 o'clock in the forenoon until you are dead. Your body is to be buried in the walls of the prison. This I pronounce for doom and the Lord have mercy on your soul'.

At the corner of the High Street and George IV Bridge there are three simple brass plates in the road. They mark the site of the last public execution in Edinburgh in 1864. The victim was called George Bryce, also known as the 'Ratho Murderer'. There is usually a plaque with these details fixed to the wall nearby, but unfortunately thieves must still be at large in Edinburgh, because each new sign which is put up seems to disappear.

Hangmen

Many famous stories have come from the countless hanging days of the past. These stories are now part of Edinburgh's folklore. The hangman was the final cog in the turning wheel of justice. Some of them officiated at hundreds of executions, making themselves notorious in their own lifetime and long afterwards. At an execution the hangman was seen by the rabble in a similar light to some football referees nowadays — the nature of the job often making him the focal point of the raw aggression of the crowd.

Mr R Chambers, in his *'Traditions of Edinburgh'*, describes a hangman of Edinburgh who was the last of a respectable family which at one time owned an estate in the South of Scotland. According to the tale he squandered his wealth and was eventually financially ruined. In order to survive he was forced to take up the 'wretched office' of public executioner. Despite his new role in society he could not forget his former social standing and, in an attempt to remind himself of better times, he would occasionally mix with the respectable citizens who played golf on Bruntsfield Links.

One evening he was recognised and a large crowd chased him from the course throwing stones and hurling abuse. The next day he was found dead at the bottom of one of the crags in Holyrood Park, said to have committed suicide because of his 'extreme degradation'. The crag was to become this 'reduced gentleman's' monument. It was known by Edinburgh folk as the Hangman's Craig.

If a hangman could cope with being a social outcast there was quite a good living to be made. The *'Edinburgh Evening Courant'* of Saturday June 13th 1789 (price 3 pence) carries an advert for a 'Common Executioner'. Any person willing to do the job was offered 'a free house with two acres of ground and a considerable salary'. There were other perks too — one hangman who used to attend church regularly was always given a pew to himself ... only because no-one would sit next to him. He was also given a separate communion after the rest of the congregation had left the church.

Finally, there was one Edinburgh hangman who received a taste of his own medicine. Alexander Cockburn was hanged by his own rope after being found guilty of the murder of a 'bluegown' or privileged beggar. One of his long time rivals, a hangman called Mackenzie, came down from Stirling to be his executioner. Would it have happened if there had been a hangman's union? Who knows.

Beheading

Although these hangmen may have prided themselves in their work, Edinburgh's most efficient executioner was not a man, but a fearsome lady, known respectfully as the 'Maiden'. She was a sturdy lass, 10 feet tall. When not carrying out her duties, she would stand idly in the High Street, patiently awaiting her next victim. Many citizens would politely bow or tip their hats as they passed by. You too can pay your respects to the Maiden. She now stands in the Royal Museum of Scotland in Chambers Street. She has kept her figure but seems a little forlorn, perhaps wistfully recalling the days when she was the centre of attraction, decapitating Scottish criminals in the Royal Mile of Edinburgh.

The Maiden was, of course, a beheading machine, a Scottish guillotine. It was first constructed in 1564 and continued to be used until 1710. The frame was made from oak and the blade was a plate of iron faced with steel which plummeted down to meet its victims with the help of more than 75 lbs of lead weight. A moveable bar between the uprights was laid on the neck preventing the criminal from withdrawing his head at the last moment.

Previously, Edinburgh had relied on the good aim of the executioner's beheading sword. Just 2 years before the Maiden came into use the 1563 Council Records show that the 'Bailies and Counsall' had ordained William Makeartney to make a 2-handed 'Heiding Sword'. No doubt Makeartney would have been pondering the loss of business in April 1565 when it was announced that Thomas Scott was to be the first to face the new and more efficient beheading machine.

The use of the 'Maiden' seems to have been indiscriminate. Men, women, rich and poor were all executed by this method. These executions usually took place in the Grassmarket, Castlehill or at the Mercat Cross. In the 1600's this merciless lady was called upon to give the kiss of death on many different occasions. Her victims include:

4th July 1600 — Jean Livingstone for murdering her husband.

20th August 1618 — Thomas Ross (minister) for forgery. Executed at the Mercat Cross.

21st January 1620 — John Duncan (baker) for killing another baker. Executed on the Castlehill.

25th February 1620 — James Reoche for horse stealing. Executed on the Castlehill.

30th September 1629 — Alex Blair, a tailor from Currie, for incest with his 'first wife's half brother's daughter'.

22nd March 1649 — The 2nd Marquis of Huntly for treason. Executed at the Mercat Cross.

20th December 1649 — James Wilson for incest committed in 1614. Executed on the Castlehill.

30th June 1661 — The First Earl of Argyle for treason. Executed at the Mercat Cross.

19th July 1678 — James Gray for murder in a duel. Executed at the Grassmarket.

The last man sentenced to meet the 'Maiden' was Robert Balfour in 1710, but he managed to escape before the execution day. But the 'Maiden's' favourite might have been Archibald the 9th Earl of Argyle, for it was he who complimented her with the now famous words 'the sweetest maiden I have ever kissed'.

Places of Punishment

Over the centuries sentences have been carried out at various sites throughout the city, all of which can still be visited today.

Grassmarket — (Below the castle on the south) — This is where I myself was launched into eternity on 27th March 1811. What an atmosphere — no wonder it was so popular for hangings. Coming down to be executed in the Grassmarket was a bit like stepping into a sports arena, such is the shape of the surrounding buildings which provided the best vantage points.

Castlehill — (Top of the Royal Mile outside the castle) — The open grassy area in front of the castle which is now the esplanade, would have been a very picturesque execution site. It was also here that young couples would sometimes go courting, although probably not on hanging days.

The Tron — (On the Royal Mile where the Tron church is today) — This was a weighing machine that stood beside the church. Many corporal punishments took place here — nailing the ear to the Tron, for example, the punishment for dishonest merchants.

Mercat Cross — (Opposite the City Chambers in the High Street) — This was once the focal point of life in Edinburgh. This is where merchants met and special announcements such as Royal proclamations were made.

Although the Mercat Cross has moved several times throughout history its vicinity has always been popular for all types of punishment, from the stocks to hangings.

Gallow Lee — (At the top of Leith Walk) — Where the Playhouse Theatre is today there was at one time just a barren piece of land. This was the Gallow Lee, situated outside the city walls between Edinburgh and Leith. Jutting out of the stark landscape was the scaffold, thin and gaunt but with a ferocious appetite.

Netherbow Port — (At the end of the High Street in the Royal Mile) — The Netherbow was one of the gateways to the city, and was demolished in 1764. The gateways were occasionally used

10

as execution sites but more often as display points for the heads, hands and other limbs of those executed. Imagine the welcome on your first visit to Edinburgh. You arrive at the City gates at dusk, and through the gloom you can make out the features of your first friendly Edinburgh face ... a head on a spike.

The Old Tolbooth — (In front of St Giles in the High Street) — This was the earliest known prison of Edinburgh. Records show that it was in existence in 1403. Although it was demolished in 1817 the outline of the building is still marked with brass plates in amongst the cobblestones. Many a prisoner spent his or her last night in the Tolbooth, but it was not designed as a long term prison. This is why, when looking at the outline, the building does not seem very large.

In those days sentencing was swift and often fatal. In 1561 a scaffold balcony was constructed against the Tolbooth at a cost of £4012 Scots. It was used to carry out many a death sentence before the Calton jail (on the site of the old Scottish Office) took over as the city prison.

Law and Order (Or the lack of it)

In the early days of Edinburgh's history, justice was maintained through the burgh courts. The difficult job of administering the law fell to the bailies. The bailies were appointed by the burgesses or town councillors who were part of a privileged group of merchants and craftsmen. While many bailies were no doubt good men, there were some appointed by influential friends who were often unfit to administer the law impartially. Many had very high opinions of themselves — one indignantly exclaimed 'I am not a man, I am a bailie!'

In 1482 King James III made the Edinburgh Provost and bailies also Sheriff and Sheriff's-deputes, so as the judicial system developed and higher courts were used in other parts of Scotland, Edinburgh still had a uniquely powerful burgh court. The burgesses could even try murder cases. The last murder trial through the burgh court was as late as 1733. Even in 1779 the historian Hugo Arnot was still expressing concern over the 'despotic' power of the Edinburgh magistrates.

As the population of Edinburgh grew, clambering down the ridge of the Royal Mile searching for space, the burgesses who carried out duties of 'watching and warding' could no longer cope. Even the ordinary merchants who were made constables by the Town Council after 1611 were not enough.

In 1679 a full time City Guard of 20 men was formed. This force was still too small so they were replaced by a well equipped Foot Company of 117 soldiers and officers. Although much more efficient they were also very expensive to maintain, and so were disbanded in 1688. The following year the unruly citizens forced the council to re-constitute the City Guard which lasted throughout the 1700's until they were replaced by a regular police force.

The Guard were mostly Highland veterans armed with a Lochaber axe, and dressed in uniforms of muddy red. The 'Toun Rats' as the populace knew them became quite famous over the years, usually for not being able to carry out their duty of preserving law and order.

In '*Heart of Midlothian*' Sir Walter Scott illustrates the problems the 'Toun Rats' were facing when dealing with the Edinburgh citizens — 'On all occasions when a holiday licensed some riot or irregularity, a skirmish with these veterans was a favourite recreation with the rabble of Edinburgh'.

The City Guard were not the first men of justice to obtain a dubious reputation in Edinburgh. 'Show me the man, and I'll show you the law' was a favourite quote of the courts in the 16th Century. In those days the outcome of your trial might ultimately depend on who you were rather than what you were.

Using friends, connections and even direct bribes were recognised and accepted ways of influencing the views of a judge. The problem was so severe that in 1579 a law was passed which prohibited 'the Lords' from taking 'brybes'. Corruption was rife and I am sure this law had little impact.

Procedure in the Courtroom would also seem strange to a present-day observer. Imagine if nowadays, before the start of a trial, bottles of strong Port were put beside the judge along with carafes of water, tumblers and biscuits. There would of course be uproar, but at one time it was a regular custom. During the course of a trial, the judge would polish off a bottle of Port 'to the great envy of the parched throats in the gallery'. This certainly casts some doubt on the truth of the well-known saying 'as sober as a judge'.

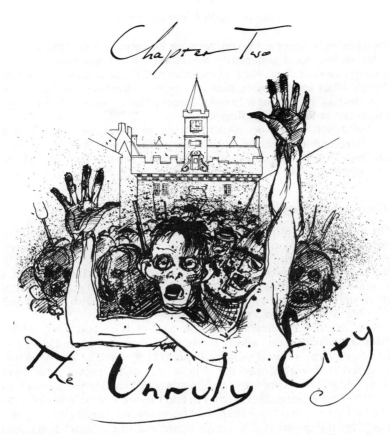

Chapter Two

The Unruly City

W hen I was a young Adam Lyal, not yet deceased, there was no flickering box in the corner of the room. It was often the unruly citizens of Edinburgh who provided our entertainment. There was something fascinating about watching the crowds gather before a riot, like dark clouds before a storm.

As young lads we amused ourselves with our own boisterous escapades, known more commonly to Edinburgh folk as 'bickers' or 'tulzies'. On the other hand, if the streets were quiet there was plenty of time for swapping dark tales of murder and mystery. In those days the Old Town seemed to reek of civil disorder.

'Bickers' were running street battles which took place in Edinburgh between the boys of different schools or different areas, Heriot's schoolboys against Watson's schoolboys, for example, or clashes between the Old Town boys and the New Town boys. The bickers took place on the borders of each other's territory and consisted mostly of stone throwing. The casualties were not too high as, despite

13

the chasing, neither side were looking for direct confrontation.

Sir Walter Scott generously described these encounters as 'only a rough kind of play'. He had experienced them as a lad in the late 1700's. They existed more than 200 years earlier however, and were reported as 'Bikkyrringis betwix Barnis'. The bickers didn't change much but at least the spelling did.

The Town Guard occasionally tried to intervene but this had the predictable effect of both sides immediately forgetting their differences and concentrating on the more satisfying targets of the uniformed Guard.

The Schoolboy Killer

On the morning of September 15th 1595, William Sinclair stood at an open window on one of the upper floors of the old Edinburgh High School. By the end of the day he was to be in jail accused of the murder of one of the city's most prominent citizens. At other windows in the building were Sinclair's fellow school pupils, most of them under the age of fourteen. Many were armed with swords and pistols and all were in a state of great excitement.

The day before, Sinclair and some other boys had gone to the Edinburgh magistrates asking for an extension to their holidays and had been flatly refused. Angry at this rebuff, some of the boys had resorted to breaking into the school that night, taking with them weapons and provisions. By morning they had barricaded themselves in. The school authorities arrived to find themselves 'barred out'. This was not for the first time; there had been several 'barring outs' in the past over the question of holidays. Sometimes these sieges had lasted more than a week.

The boys were all in high spirits as they rained shouts of defiance on the adults below. The Rector, Hercules Rollock, tried to reason with them but they were not to be swayed. When it was obvious no headway was being made, extra help was called for. The council sent Bailie John McMorane, one of the wealthiest merchants in Edinburgh. As a bailie one of his jobs was to help maintain law and order in the city.

McMorane demanded the boys surrender but they were in no mood for giving up without conditions. It was decided to break the door down and enter by force rather than getting involved in a long siege. As the boys looked down they could see the Bailie's assistants battering the door. It wasn't long before they could hear the wood beginning to splinter and give way. The boys were now becoming desperate; some of them threatened to open fire if the assault con-tinued. Inside the building there was great confusion and agitation.

14

At some point just before the door gave way, Sinclair stepped up to the window, leaned out and fired his pistol at the group below.

The effect was devastating, outside Bailie McMorane lay dead on the ground. Everyone was stunned, work on the door stopped, and the boys ceased their clamouring. No-one had suspected that the rowdy action of the schoolboys would ever lead to murder. People rushed to the scene from all directions. The boys now put up little resistance and were soon led away to be locked up in the Tolbooth. William Sinclair and 7 others went to trial but never stood on the scaffold; they were all acquitted by the 'express warrant' of King James VI.

Part of the reason must have been the very young age of the culprits ... but they were also sons of wealthy and powerful families. Sinclair's father was none other than the Chancellor of Caithness.

So the boys went free and the incident went down in history as the last 'barring out'. Hercules Rollock was sacked and it was years before the school began to regain its prestige. The school exists to this day, and the present Rector still enjoys reading out at the beginning of each session the 30 or so old School Rules. They were written one and a half centuries ago and contain rule XVII: 'No gunpowder, fireworks or firearms of any description are permitted to be brought within the grounds'.

As for William Sinclair, in his later years he was to become Sir William Sinclair of Mey. Obviously the events of his school days did not adversely affect his career. This of course in no way suggests that if any of the present boys were to shoot a magistrate they could increase their chances of obtaining a knighthood!

The Snowball Riot

Scotland is not always hot and sunny...

Sometimes in the winter there is quite a lot of snow. As every schoolchild knows it is a great time for snowball fights — a rare opportunity to throw a missile at your least favourite person (teacher) and still remain anonymous.

These actions may seem harmless, but things were different in 1870. On a cold February morning of that year, some high-spirited

Edinburgh University students began throwing snowballs at passers-by on the South Bridge. It was all innocent fun until the appearance of a strong body of police at mid-day. This transformed the scene into what the 'Scotsman' newspapers later described as a 'Serious Snowball Riot at the University'.

The students had prepared 'an abundance of ammunition in the shape of snowballs'. They now took great delight in launching them at the police. The barrage was so great that the police were forced to retreat. Wild cheers from the rioters were short-lived as the police mounted a second, more determined charge.

The students simply retreated into the University. Once the gates were locked they were able to continue throwing snowballs at the unamused 'defenders of the peace' who were frustrated in their attempts to retaliate.

Between 1-2pm classes at the Surgeons Hall were dismissed and they too joined in the pelting of passers-by. More police were called for and soon two fresh bodies of constables arrived. Despite being under concentrated fire they bravely decided to launch a final attack on the student fortress. One division entered the compound by a rear gate, the second attacked the main gate. This proved to be the decisive tactic of the battle. The truncheons defeated the snowballs and 13 prisoners were taken.

The large crowd who had earlier been pelted by the students now began jeering the police as they marched their prisoners off to the Police Office. Some continued to throw snowballs and the police made two or three charges into the crowd. They only succeeded in capturing one 'diminutive urchin' which brought even more derision from the crowd, and caused great embarrassment for the police.

As darkness fell and people made their way homeward, activity died away and there was peace at last. After all the efforts of the police the students who had been charged with breach of the peace pleaded 'not guilty' and were released by the courts. Over the next few days there were no further reports of snowball challenges by the students. All opposition seemed to have melted away.

Trades Violence

In the old days the Town Council of Edinburgh consisted of merchants and tradesmen and there was always a battle for power between the two groups. To combat the increasing influence of the merchants the tradesmen formed themselves into 'Incorporations' ie — Bakers, Candlemakers, Wrights, Stonemasons, Fleschers (Butchers), Cordiners (Shoemakers) and so on. These tradesmen were quick to act if they felt that one of their own had been unjustly treated.

In 1560, when strict legislation was passed concerning adultery, one of the first to fall foul of the new laws was the Deacon of Fleschers (Head of the Butchers). He was sentenced to be bound and carted through the streets of the town so that all could witness his disgrace. It is not certain what the trades incorporations thought of the crime but it is clear that they resented the indignity of the punishment bestowed upon one of their most prominent leaders. Their reaction was simple enough. They banded together, broke into the Tolbooth and set the man free. The authorities were powerless to resist such an aggressive reaction and in the end the sentence was never carried out. This of course does not mean that the incorporations condoned the sins of the Flescher.

Another example of the trades taking the law into their own hands occurred after James Gillan, a shoemaker's servant, was sentenced to death for taking part in a banned parade. When the day of execution arrived the tradesmen rose up and attacked the Tolbooth prison. Armed with axes and a battering ram, they easily broke in. (Practice makes perfect?). The guards were overpowered and the crowd released James Gillan and just to show their contempt of the authorities, freed all the other prisoners as well. The Provost and the Bailies watched helplessly as the whole event progressed into what was recorded as 'a general riot."

Mob Rule

Edinburgh was once described by King James VI of Scotland as 'an unfit place for the ministration of justice'. His angry remarks about his own capital city came after being forced out of town by widespread rioting. These riots were spontaneous outbursts by the Edinburgh populace usually challenging some aspect of the authority of the day. The vehemence of these eruptions was intensified by the fact that the population were hemmed in by the city walls and the Nor'Loch. The Old Town was a densely populated area in which the lives of the rich and powerful overlapped with the poor and insignificant much more than in any other city at that time. Everyone knew everyone else's business. Once aroused by some perceived injustice, there was little the Magistrates or Town Guards could do to quell the anger of the Edinburgh citizens. The best thing was to stand back and let the storm blow itself out. This seething mass of volatile public opinion was known as the 'Edinburgh Mob'.

General Joe

Joseph Smith was a man who managed to harness the power of

the 'mob'. Despite being a lowly cobbler and having a stooped and deformed physique he had the gift of arousing and manipulating a crowd. Over the years his position as unofficial leader of the mob grew stronger and stronger and eventually he became known to one and all as 'General Joe'. His summons was the beat of his drum and it was claimed that his signal could bring 10,000 to the streets of Edinburgh, all ready to follow his lead in righting some wrong.

In the 1770's there was a shortage of grain in the city and as a result the prices began to rise above the reach of many common folk. The reaction of General Joe is a typical example of his influence. He and his cronies decided to rouse the mob in protest. Thousands thronged the streets shouting and cheering, a wild orchestra of noise, Joseph leading them with his drum. They marched from dealer to dealer threatening violence and demanding that they sell their meal at an agreed lower price. All wisely complied except for a merchant in the Grassmarket who boasted later to his colleagues that he had outwitted General Joe by using false measures when weighing out the meal, thereby cutting his losses.

But word got out and when Joseph and the mob returned, they were in an angry mood. The dealer was given a beating and forced to re-pay the difference to those he had cheated. The mob then sacked his shop for good measure, or for bad measure depending on how you look at it.

Because of General Joe's influence the council were constantly calling on him to mediate in riot situations. He must have been well aware of the power he wielded but did not seem to abuse it to his own end. Joseph's reign over the Edinburgh mob ended in 1780. Every general has his weakness and Joseph's was alcohol. His fall from his high position came from a fall from another high position. He got very drunk one day at the races in Leith and when coming home fell off the stagecoach and was killed. The Magistrates sincerely hoped 'we ne'er shall look upon his like again'.

Porteous Riots

In 1736 the Edinburgh mob caused outrage in the government and put the city to shame in the eyes of the whole of Britain. It all started before the execution of a smuggler named Andrew Wilson. Sentence was to be carried out on April 14th 1736 and during the weeks beforehand angry mutterings could be heard in the closes and wynds. Wilson had aroused a lot of public sympathy by allegedly holding back the guards while his accomplice George Robertson made his escape during their last church service.

When the execution day for this newfound 'hero' arrived there was tension in the air. The mob were in belligerent mood as thousands of people began to fill the Grassmarket to witness the hanging.

The magistrates were well aware of the rumblings but were determined that order would be kept. The man entrusted with this task was Captain John Porteous of the Town Guard. The Council appreciated his firm hand and guards and public alike feared his harshness and violent temper.

He was a well known character and gossip flowed (true and false) about his brutality.

Captain Porteous was said to have been in a foul mood on the hanging day because the Council had taken the extra precaution of lining the route to the Grassmarket with soldiers. Porteous resented this, seeing it as undermining his authority and questioning the capabilities of the Town Guard.

In actual fact (and unfortunately for Wilson) there was no trouble before or during the execution. But as the hangman went to cut down the body some of the crowd who had been standing in sullen silence started throwing stones and mud. To most onlookers this was no more than usual, but it must be said that later accounts do describe varying levels of provocation.

Captain Porteous began to get angry. Some witnesses alleged he had been drinking while others claimed he was still furious about the use of the soldiers. The general view was expressed by one 14 year old eye-witness: Porteous 'inflamed with wine and jealousy, thought it proper to order his Guard to fire, their muskets being loaded'.

The Guard hesitated, so Porteous again bellowed his order that they should fire on the crowd. Shots rang out and people fell to the ground screaming. There was complete confusion. Some of the guard fired above the crowd but this act of mercy only meant that many watching from windows were wounded and one 'unfortunate lad' was killed outright.

There was first panic then anger and the retreating Guard were chased up the West Bow where they again fired on the incensed mob. At the end of it all 9 people lay dead and many more were wounded.

The fury of the citizens did not abate in the next few days and the Town Council came under great pressure to deal decisively with the Town Guard who by now had been branded as 'murderers'. Captain Porteous and 30 of his men were arrested and put on trial for firing on the crowd 'without any just cause or necessary occasion'.

The case was fraught with claims and counter-claims. Porteous was made out to be the villain of the piece, but his lawyers questioned just how firm had he been instructed to be by his superiors. The Crown produced 28 witnesses to give evidence against the Captain but Porteous was able to call on 16 witnesses to contradict the prosecution's version of events. At the end of a stormy trial he was found guilty by only one vote.

This was enough for those who looked forward to his execution day on the 7th of September. However, there were those who felt Porteous had been a scapegoat and did not believe his sentence to be fair. Friends in high places lobbied on his behalf and Queen Caroline was persuaded on the 2nd of September to offer a 6 week reprieve. This was not a pardon but in Edinburgh it was seen as the prelude to one. After this the word got out that there was going to be a hanging, reprieve or no reprieve.

The morning of his original hanging date (September 7th) passed uneventfully and Porteous was able to remain in his cell rather than face the gallows. His fortunes were to be short-lived (literally). That same evening what seems to have been a well organised and thought out plan was put in motion.

A small but determined group of people took over the City gates to prevent any of the soldiers stationed in the Canongate from entering the town. This small group swelled as they marched on the Guard House in the High Street where the Guard were overpowered and disarmed. Then they moved on to the Tolbooth prison. The door was burnt down and Porteous hauled from his cell. By now there were thousands of people of all ages, some still wearing their night-clothes, surging down the steep West Bow towards the Grassmarket.

Captain Porteous was hung from a dryers pole 10 feet off the ground. There are romantic tales of the crowds acting in an uncanny silence and with great decorum. The more likely versions tell of how Porteous was twice let down and hung up again while the crowd jeered and some hacked at him with axes.

When the rest of the country learned of the mob's actions on that night, there was an outcry. How was it that law and order could so easily be flaunted? Who was responsible? There was even a motion put to the House of Commons that Edinburgh's Lord Provost should be imprisoned, the city gates destroyed and Edinburgh's Town Guard disbanded in disgrace.

These measures never came to pass and the enquiry set up after the lynching met with a wall of silence. To this day nobody knows who the ringleaders were. Once again the potential force available to anyone who could harness and manipulate the power of Edinburgh's mob had been amply demonstrated.

The Blue Blanket

I'd like to continue on a more positive note. In 1482 King James III was being held captive in Edinburgh Castle. He was rescued by a force who had the spirited help of many Edinburgh citizens.

Because the mob had risen to his aid James III granted the trades a banner which was to be used when rallying the townsfolk to defend their king, country or their own right. It became known as the 'Blue Blanket' and what is believed to be the original is now in The Royal Scottish Museum in Chambers Street. A record of the mob being recognised for their fierce unity.

The Original Dr Jekyll and Mr Hyde

Many feel that Deacon Brodie, an 18th Century character, gave Robert Louis Stevenson the inspiration to write his famous novel 'Dr Jekyll and Mr Hyde'. The story of Brodie himself will explain the connection.

William Brodie came from a well respected Edinburgh family. His father was a prosperous cabinet maker who was also Deacon of the Incorporation of Wrights (carpenters and other tradesmen) and a member of the Town Council. Young Brodie was to follow his father's footsteps into business and ultimately on to the Town Council as a Deacon in 1781. By now he too was wealthy and when his father died he inherited a fortune and the family home in the Lawnmarket. Deacon Brodie rubbed shoulders with all the high society of the day. He was even a member of the exclusive Cape Club which had some of Edinburgh's leading citizens amongst its members.

So if this was the Dr Jekyll in his character who was the Mr Hyde?

Brodie was a gambler and wagered large amounts on the popular cock-fights of his day. All night he made merry in the dark corners and dens of the city with many a dubious character. He had two mistresses and numerous illegitimate offspring. This was understandably very expensive and no doubt it was cash flow problems that turned him to crime. Or was it perhaps the Hyde in his character, the part of him that loved the taste of danger and the flavour of chance?

For a long time his night-time line of work proved to be very successful. Other burglars did not have the advantage of knowing their victims so well. During his daily work he was able to obtain clay impressions of his clients' keys and make copies of them. With these duplicates Deacon Brodie could pay a second visit to his clients, this time as a burglar, thief and rogue.

Despite so many spectacular robberies from various houses and shops he remained above suspicion, protected by a cloak of respectability. One wonders what he must have been thinking when he attended a meeting called by the Town Council to discuss the sudden increase in burglaries. Did he make any well informed suggestions to the other councillors?

Brodie's confidence must have been growing because he now took on three accomplices: Andrew Ainslie, George Smith and John Brown. They were casual acquaintances from the low taverns and gambling dens. With Brodie as their ringleader they were able to carry out many daring raids including the theft of the Edinburgh University Silver Mace.

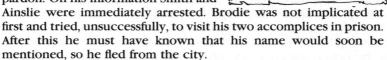

In a later break-in they stole a large quantity of very valuable silk from a High Street trader. This led to the offer of a free pardon to any accomplice who was willing to come forward with any information.

It was a bungled attempt to rob the Excise Office of Scotland on the 5th of March 1788 that led to Brown turning informer in exchange for the free pardon. On his information Smith and Ainslie were immediately arrested. Brodie was not implicated at first and tried, unsuccessfully, to visit his two accomplices in prison. After this he must have known that his name would soon be mentioned, so he fled from the city.

On the 14th of March 1788 the *'Edinburgh Evening Courant'* carried a notice announcing a £200 reward for 'William Brodie, a confiderable Houfe Carpenter and Burgefs of the City of Edinburgh'. The description of Brodie was very graphic and is delightful to read nowadays — here is the introduction (in some cases f is an s).

'William Brodie is about 5 feet 4 inches; is about forty-eight years of age but looks rather younger than he is; broad over the shoulders and very fmall over the loins; has dark brown full eyes with large black eye-brows; under the right eye there is the fcar of a cut, which is ftill a little fore at the point of the eye next to the nose, a fallow complexion; a particular motion with his mouth and lips when he fpeaks, which he does full and flow, his mouth becoming commonly open at the time; and his tongue doubling up as it were, fhews itself towards the roof of his mouth;...'

Deacon Brodie made his escape to Holland where he hoped to take a sailing ship to America and freedom. Unfortunately some letters he sent home allowed him to be traced. Before the ship set sail Brodie was captured and returned to Edinburgh as a prisoner.

Brodie and Smith went on trial together, Brown and Ainslie giving evidence against them. They were found guilty and sentenced to be hanged on October 1st 1788. A member of the jury, William Creech, Robert Burns' publisher wrote an account of the trial but delayed its publication 'in order to give an account of the behaviour of the criminals at their execution'.

On the 17th of September 1788 Deacon Brodie wrote to the Lord Provost, magistrates and council of Edinburgh, appealing for the death sentence to be commuted to transportation to Botany Bay in Australia. He also asked them to draw their attention 'to the infamous character of the two principal witnesses' who were brought against him. It was all to no avail.

After 34 days in captivity awaiting his execution he was led from the prison to the scaffold. It was erected in front of St Giles Church only a stone's throw away from Brodie's house in what is now called Brodie's Close. Four friends were present as requested so that his body might be handed over to be 'decently draped' and interred.

In front of a huge crowd he left this world — hung, ironically, on the city's new gallows which he himself had designed.

Many leaflets and pamphlets were produced concerning Brodie's misdeeds, trial and execution. Perhaps the simplest obituary, however, came from his friends at the Cape Club. In the manuscript 'List of Members' opposite the name of William Brodie has been drawn a scaffold with a body suspended from it and the words '1st October 1788, for robbing Excise'. A succint last comment to mark the demise of the original Dr Jekyll and Mr Hyde.

The Guardians of the City

The usefu' Cadie plies in Street,
To bide the Profits o' his Feet
For by thir Lads Auld Reikie's Fock
Ken but a SAMPLE o' the Stock
O' thieves that mighty wad oppress,
And maik baith Goods and gear the less.

(Robert Ferguson)

While out trying to 'maik baith Goods and gear the less', people like Deacon Brodie and I had to keep one eye open for the 'Cadies'.

They took messages, ran errands, acted as guides and would perform any job that required a comprehensive knowledge of the city. Not much escaped their notice and this was, for us, the dangerous aspect of their talents.

The magistrates often called upon the Cadies to help with difficult cases, especially in the days before forensic evidence when the authorities relied heavily on information received to solve crimes. Major Topham who visited Edinburgh in the 18th Century described the Cadies: 'it is entirely owing to them that there are fewer robberies and less housebreakings in Edinburgh than anywhere else'.

There are still Cadies in Edinburgh today 'biding the profits of their feet'. The 'Cadies Scottish Personal Guides' operate excellent walking tours in the Old Town. They like to think that one of Major Topham's observations is still accurate, 'poor but marvellously honest'.

In addition to the Cadies there was another factor which helped to keep the crime rate down. The Old Town was one of the most densely populated areas in the whole of Europe. Everyone knew everyone else's business and as soon as a stranger came down a close eyes and ears recorded every detail. The whispered gossip sounded louder than any burglar alarm. This was a real 'neighbourhood watch scheme' which nowadays is being encouraged again.

It must have been effective because William Creech (in his *Fugitive Pieces*') states that in the winter of 1790-91 'there was not a robbery, housebreaking, nor a theft publicly known to the amount of forty shillings within the City of Edinburgh'.

The Trial of the Body Snatchers

'No trial in the memory of any man now living has excited so deep, universal and appalling an interest'. So quoted the Edinburgh Observer on Wednesday the 24th of December 1828. The case became famous throughout Britain and concerns two of Edinburgh's most notorious characters, William Burke and William Hare. They had been brought to court to face charges involving the sale of bodies for medical research.

This was not a new thing. As early as 1738 it was recorded that the recently departed were leaving the quiet graveyards to enter into the lively discussions of the city's anatomy classes. The opinions of these former citizens were not considered, however, as they were dissected in the name of science on the slabs of the Edinburgh Medical Schools.

In the early 1800's the study of anatomy in Edinburgh surged forward. Surgeons like Dr Robert Knox could attract as many as 500 people to their anatomy classes. The students came from all walks of life, young doctors, artists, lawyers and 'men of letters'.

Officially each medical school was only allowed the body of one executed criminal per year. This did not meet the demands of the anatomy students, so there arose the sinister trade of the 'body snatchers'.

In many graveyards on dark moonless nights, figures could be seen flitting amongst the gravestones, going about their gory business. These suspicious characters were often the medical students themselves trying to ensure a fresh supply to their own classes. This ability to raise the dead gave the body snatchers another nickname popular at the time — 'resurrectionists'.

This practice so horrified the general public that watchtowers were constructed in some Edinburgh graveyards to protect those recently buried from exhumation. In addition to the towers, protective walls and iron bars can still be seen around some old Edinburgh graves.

But William Burke and William Hare were not hindered by these precautions. Their victims were the waifs and strays of the Old Town, people whom nobody would miss. They would be lured from the streets to their deaths and then their bodies would be sold to the medical schools. To this day nobody knows exactly how many disappeared, but the estimates at the time ran somewhere between 13 and 30.

The trial began on Wednesday 17th December 1828. It was a cold clear morning and by 8 am a huge crowd had gathered outside the High Courts behind St Giles in the Royal Mile. The crowd stood patiently waiting to be allowed in, stamping their feet, trying to stay warm. As they swapped opinions on the case the police cordoned

off the area in order to prevent any disturbances. Just before 8 am the Press were allowed in and then the public galleries were quickly filled.

Many hundreds were turned away disappointed. It was 9.40 am by the time everyone had settled down and the Jury was brought in. The Jury was followed by the two accused who were placed at the bar. The trial began at 10.15 am.

Since there was a lack of evidence on the other alleged murders, the case centred around the details given concerning the demise of an old Irishwoman Mrs Docherty. In fact the case was so weak that to ensure a conviction William Hare and his wife were not to face charges. Instead they gave evidence on behalf of the Crown against William Burke as well as against the woman he had lived with for some time, Helen McDougal.

As he entered the courtroom Burke was described as being a man 'below middle size, but stoutly made. He had hair and whiskers of a sandy colour and sunken eyes'. This was by no stretch of the imagination a particularly evil looking man, but the observant 'Observer' reporter noted 'there is a hardness about the features, mixed with an expression in the grey twinkling eyes far from inviting'.

The same reporter described Helen McDougal as 'thin and spare made', with the 'ordinary look of extreme poverty and misery common to the unfortunate individuals of the same degraded class'. He did remark generously, however, that dressed in her shabby cotton gown and brown silk bonnet 'we are inclined to think she presents the remains of feminine comeliness'.

As the case progressed the story of Mrs Docherty unravelled. She had only recently arrived in Edinburgh from Ireland and was befriended by Burke in a shop. According to the testimony of the shop boy Burke claimed he was related to the woman and offered her breakfast in his lodging house. His plan must have been clear in his mind because later on in the day he asked his two lodgers Mr and Mrs Gray to move out and stay somewhere else at his expense. A cost presumably soon to be recovered.

Mrs Gray returned with her husband the next morning and, being suspicious of the goings on, asked for Mrs Docherty. She was not satisfied with the reply that the woman had been evicted for being rude nor was she happy with Burke's warning to keep away from the straw bedding. Indeed this merely fuelled her inquisitiveness and at the first opportunity she investigated the bedding and found underneath the straw the murdered old woman. Mrs Gray testified that Burke was not there at that moment. She also testified that Helen McDougal had promised her £10 to keep quiet about the whole ghastly business. Mrs Gray and her husband were not tempted despite the large bribe and soon the police were informed and investigations began.

There were excited murmurs and strained necks in the packed courtroom as David Paterson, a very important witness, took the stand. He was keeper of Dr Knox's museum at the medical school.

He said that he had gone to the lodging house and been told by Burke that 'he had procured something for the Doctor and pointed to the head of a bed where some straw was lying'. Nothing was shown but he understood. Perhaps this was a practised routine.

On November 1st at 9am Burke went to visit Dr Knox and at 7pm that evening, Paterson was instructed to receive a consignment from Burke and Hare. They arrived with a porter who had carried the body up in an old tea-chest. Ironically Burke had purchased the temporary coffin for Mrs Docherty in the same shop that he had first befriended her.

Dr Knox had given Paterson £5 to split amongst the trio, the balance of £8 to be paid in a few days. At this point Paterson told a hushed courtroom that Dr Knox had had other dealings with Burke and Hare and they frequently brought bodies to the lecture rooms and stated that he supposed 'they had never been interred'.

All this evidence was supported by the contributions of various neighbours and the police reports.

William Hare and his wife were then called on to confirm the events. They both accused Burke, saying he alone had suffocated Mrs Docherty. Many believed that Hare had not been an idle bystander and the use of these witnesses caused great scandal in itself. In summing up, Mr Cockburn, one of the defending lawyers, attacked the use of such dubious characters.

He said he had often heard of this type of 'King's evidence' but never 'persons coming to give evidence with other serious crimes over their heads, the very idea was horrible'.

Despite these accusations the Lord Justice Clerk felt that the information given by these witnesses could be 'sifted'. William Hare gave them plenty to sift, always knowing that at the end of the trial his wife would be released and he himself would be guaranteed a safe passage out of Scotland. It was believed that he later settled in London.

After both sides had finished their final summings up, the case drew to a close. It was 8.30am on the Thursday morning and almost 24 hours had passed since the remarkable trial began. Even the Lord Provost of Edinburgh had attended. Like almost everyone else he had stayed from beginning to end, fascinated by the revelations.

In another room the Jury of 15 men discussed the evidence and in just under an hour returned to give their verdicts. William Burke was found 'guilty' of the murder of Mrs Docherty and Helen McDougal 'not proven'.

Before passing sentence one of the 4 judges, Lord Meadowbank, summarized the case. He pointed out the calculated evilness of Burke's pre-meditated murder. Having quickly established that the old woman was new to Edinburgh and little known around town, Burke lured her into his trust with the empty promise of friendship.

In reality he knew he had found another victim, another body to be laid out for dissection at the medical school with no questions asked. In the busy streets of a crowded old town she would not be missed and William Burke would be free to plan his next profitable murder.

Lord Meadowbank considered it all 'one of the most monstrous exhibitions of atrocity ever disclosed in the annals of criminal jurisprudence'. He sentenced Burke to 'suffer death on the scaffold on the 28th day of January next' (1829).

The Lord Justice Clerk warned Burke to prepare his mind 'in the most suitable manner to appear in a very short time before the Throne of Almighty God to answer for this crime'.

The courtroom emptied. The news of the verdict spread among the hundreds waiting outside. Soon the story of the case reverberated throughout the city and far beyond. Hare had cheated the gallows and sped to England, and was never seen again. Dr Knox was never charged but public opinion forced him to leave Edinburgh, his promising career ruined. In the end it was only William Burke who bore the full weight of the law, hanged in the High Street in front of 25,000 people. Ironically, as Lord Meadowbank had instructed, Burke's body was 'given for dissection'. Thus Burke helped further the advance of medical science in exactly the same fashion as all his victims.

It was a notorious case at the time, but few could have guessed that Burke and Hare would enter into Scotland's folklore. For many years children's voices would echo the story between the tall buildings in their chant:

'Doon the close and up the stair
But an' ben wi' Burke an' Hare
Burke's the butcher
Hare's the thief
Knox the man who buys the beef'!

So Burke and Hare are still with us more than a century and a half later. Burke is still with us in a physical sense — to this day his skeleton can be seen at the Medical School. It was to be displayed, in the words of Lord Meadowbank, 'in order that posterity may keep in remembrance these atrocious crimes'.

Chapter Three

Plague and Disaster

Many types of disease persisted in Edinburgh because of notoriously bad sanitary conditions. 'Gardy Loo!' was a popular cry with Edinburgh citizens. It was a warning shout and was their pronunciation of the French 'Gardez l'eau', meaning 'watch out for the water' There was only one problem — it wasn't just water. All manner of filth imaginable was thrown out into the streets and would gather into great stinking mounds all around the town.

An Englishman, Sir William Brereton, visited Edinburgh in 1636. He described the city as 'a most healthful place to live in, were not the inhabitants the most nasty and slothful people. I could never pass through the hall but was constrained to hold my nose'.

In the very early 1700's Edinburgh was seen through the eyes of another visitor, Captain Edward Burt. He was a bit more graphic as he described his journey home to where he was staying while in the capital city:

29

'Being in my Retreat to pass through a long narrow Wynd or Alley, to my new Lodgings, a guide was assigned to me, who went before me to prevent my Disgrace, crying out all the Way, with a loud Voice, 'Hud your Haunde'. The opening up of a Sash, or otherwise opening a Window, made me tremble, while behind and before me, at some little Distance, fell the terrible Shower.'

'Well I escaped all the Danger, and arrived, not only safe and sound, but sweet and clean, at my new Quarters; but when I was in bed I was forced to hide my Head between the Sheets; for the Smell of the Filth, thrown out by the Neighbours on the Back-side of the House, came pouring into the Room to such a Degree, I was almost poisoned by the Stench'.

So although both men reported enjoying excellent hospitality from the people themselves, neither were impressed with their living conditions. Who knows how many Edinburgh citizens must have died from diseases resulting from the cry of 'Gardy Loo!'

Plague!

Unlike Sir William Brereton and Captain Burt, there was never a more unwelcome visitor to the capital city than the dreaded 'pestelens' or plague. The announcement of its arrival struck fear and apprehension into every heart, rich or poor. Whole families would pack up and disappear through the City gates and those who had to stay prayed fervently that none of their kin would fall victim to this merciless killer.

If a household was struck by the plague, the family had to warn others by displaying a white rag at the window. At first there would only be a few dashes of white, but as the plague spread, these rags seemed to flutter everywhere. Slowly the city surrendered. The busy markets and street corners became quiet and deserted. Normally bustling closes were empty except for the 'foule clengers' — men who wore ominous black cloaks with white St Andrews Crosses, and were responsible for the 'disinfection' of stricken households. These houses were thoroughly washed and then the 'clengers' set fire to heather, whin and straw in the rooms. This method of 'smoking' a building was used because it was believed the plague was a venomous quality in the air which could penetrate and adhere to all sorts of materials depending on their porosity. In the early stages of infection in the city, the bodies of the dead were gathered at night. Creaking carts with bells attached lurched along under the cloak of darkness. It wasn't long before so many people were dying that these carts were seen out on the streets during the day; no point in sparing sensitive minds when all were numbed by the death toll as it inexorably rose every day, every week, every month.

Because townsfolk were so terrified of the spread of the plague the punishments for breaking the regulations could be very harsh.

On the 18th of February 1530 Margaret Cook was found guilty of theft. An additional charge considered more serious was that she had entered the city after travelling from 'Sanctandros' (not a Greek island, but actually St Andrews), which was infected by the plague. For these crimes she was branded on both cheeks, her clothes burnt and herself banished from the town '...for all ye dayis of hir lyf...'

In the same year Marion Clerk was accused of concealing the fact that she had the plague and still passed among the townsfolk causing the risk of infection. She was sentenced to be drowned in a quarry hole, or as the court said '...adingit to be had to ye quarrel hollis and yair to be dronit quhill scho be deid'.

The tale of David Duly is perhaps the best known story concerning the plague in Edinburgh. This man was to survive not only the plague but also the sentence of death by hanging.

David Duly was a tailor whose wife fell ill during the plague of 1530 but he did not report this to the authorities until after she had died. It came to light that during this time he had gone to St Giles Kirk in the High Street to pray for his family 'amangis ye cleyne pepill'. So when the 'clean people' found out he had nearly 'infekkit all ye toune' he was sentenced on the 2nd of August 1530 to be hanged before his own door. But this story does have a happy ending. He 'eschapit' with his life because the rope broke. The Council decided that because he was a poor man with lots of children he should be spared. But the seriousness of this crime could not be ignored so he and his family were banished from Edinburgh for ever (some say he was sent to Glasgow because that was the worst thing they could think of).

The Last Great Plague

In the year 1645, Edinburgh was ravaged by the last but also the most severe of all its plagues. It was believed to have come from

Newcastle after an outbreak there in October 1644. By December the Town Council of Edinburgh were taking the usual precautions.

When a ship arrived from Newcastle or one of the 'suspected places' it was not allowed to discharge any cargo and the passengers were prevented from disembarking.

In some cases if there were no signs or history of the plague on board, the ship's Captain would be allowed to unload. This was on the rather risky agreement that if his goods were to cause an outbreak of infection they could be confiscated and he himself put to death.

Islands in the Firth of Forth near Edinburgh were used for 'detention and disinfection'. At Inchcolm, ships were deliberately scuttled or 'bored' before being refloated and cleaned. No doubt the crew were bored too as quarantine could be anything up to 40 days. These time consuming and expensive regulations meant that many tried to avoid them by smuggling goods to land all along the coast. The punishment for this was death and citizens hoarding such goods could be banished from the city.

Events of 1644–47

December 1644 — Despite all precautions, the plague breaks out around Christmas.

31st March 1645 — The Council are so worried by the spread of the plague that gatherings after weddings and funerals are banned. The wearing of plaids is also prohibited (this may seem strange, but it was necessary as a plaid could effectively conceal the signs of infection).

10th April 1645 — The Town Council order that the graduation ceremony at the College should be brought forward. Many students and their families leave the city.

July 1645 — The Court of Session and the Scottish Parliament leave Edinburgh. Parliament meets in Stirling.

August 1645 — The city begins to suffer from food shortages.

September 1645 — The outbreaks decrease, it seems the worst has passed.

27th October 1645 — Council and magistrates are ordered to return to the city; many do not.

19th November 1645 — The Edinburgh College resumes in Linlithgow because 'thair is no appearance that the people can be moved to send their children to this Town' (Edinburgh).

January 1646 — Fresh cases no longer being reported.

April 1646 — Houses from which the last infected were removed are being re-opened.

After more than a year of suffering the town is beginning to recover.

3rd December 1646 — 2421 people are reported to have died of the plague in Leith, more than half the population. 'The number of the dead exceeds the number of the living'.

January 1647 — It is not known how many perished in Edinburgh itself, but financial losses are calculated to be 10,792 pounds, 6 shillings and 8 pence.

'Fire!'

'See the red snaw!' Was an Aberdonian's exclamation at one of the terrible fires in Edinburgh. To him the millions of sparks flying through the air seemed like falling snow.

The threat of fire in the city was always a well-recognised one. In 1426 merchants who sold hay, straw, heather and lint, had to illuminate their premises with lanterns rather than candles. It was also forbidden to carry a naked flame from one building to another.

Almost all the houses at this time had thatched roofs. It was not until the *'Edinburgh Improvement Act of 1621'* that it was ordered that buildings should be roofed with lead, slate, tile or stone, to try and reduce the fire hazard.

As the Old Town became more and more densely populated the risk of fire grew. With buildings standing so close together it was very difficult to stop the flames spreading, especially in a city famous for being so windy.

The water required for fire-fighting was limited. There were 'fire points' on the pipes between the city wells but these were inadequate. Finally, on April 21st 1703, after terrible fires in 1700, the first 'Company for Quenching of Fire' was formed. There were to be 12 firemasters, each with 6 assistants, and 300 leather buckets. This was still a part-time, unprofessional, untrained band of men who lacked co-ordination and leadership.

One reason for lack of action was due to the belief held by many people that great fires were sent by God as a punishment for sins. Some ministers preached to this effect from the pulpit. Some took it further — Elizabeth Wast claimed that the fires of 1700 had been sent specifically to punish Sabbath-breaking. She said that there had been signs that they were imminent. On one Sunday a smell of burning lingered in the High Street, which was so strong that people went from house to house searching for the source. They found nothing but a week later the fire arrived and they had to flee for their lives.

One interesting type of fireman, mentioned in the 1703 'Rules to be Observed by Inhabitants', was the city muck-man. Besides cleaning out the closes he was asked to attend all fires. Because of the lack of water his job was to dash to the scene with creels of 'muck', usually horse dung. Once thrown on the fire, the dung gave off ammonia fumes which acted as a natural chemical fire-extinguisher.

A few ill-judged throws from your coll-eagues, and being an 'all natural' fireman could get very messy. Before the first town fire brigades, householders could protect their properties by approaching fire-insurance companies. Policy holders were issued with metal plates called 'Firemarks', to be displayed on the front of the insured building. These plates were brightly coloured so they would stand out (in a fire?) and were decorated with the company logo. At first these companies had salvage teams but these groups evolved into untrained fire-fighters armed with more modern equipment.

There was one glaring weakness. When it came to the safety of the whole town these companies had no statutory obligation to put out fires in properties not insured with them. Imagine, if you will, 15 to 20 men standing in front of a blazing tenement. They watch the flames devouring the building. If we look closer at the faces of these men, lit by the flames of the fire, we observe their happy, confident, satisfied smiles. This building was not insured by one of 'their' companies. But what about the anger and frustration on those same faces when sometimes they discovered that several companies had policy-holders in the same tenement! Arguments over water would come to blows and accusations were made about the deliberate sabotage of equipment.

Baptism of Fire

By the early 1800's there was growing discontent with the insurance arrangements. After bad fires in 1811, 1813 and June 1824, the Police Commissioners and the insurance companies met to discuss a new fire fighting force. On the 10th of October 1824 they had agreed to form the Edinburgh Municipal Fire Brigade, a body of 80 men with their own firemaster — a young man called James Braidwood. They too might have been destined to mediocrity had it not been for their ruthless 'baptism of fire' which showed exactly the importance of changes.

On Monday, 15th of November 1824 at 10 pm, fire broke out in a large 7 storey tenement in Old Assembly Close. The fire raged all night destroying most of the buildings in that area as far as the Cowgate. All 22 of the insurance companies' engines were in attendance as were the soldiers of the Castle.

They fought to control the blaze. Through the smoke and the searing heat they had to contend with great piles of belongings hoarded into the middle of the street. Sparks flew everywhere. As one historian said 'their appearance was like the thickest drift of a snowstorm'.

Thousands gathered to watch, including many dignitaries. Sir Walter Scott observed the 'conflagration' from the steeple of St Giles.

The fire lulled but on Tuesday morning embers in the Tron Kirk steeple ignited and shortly afterwards the bell came crashing down. Molten lead could be seen dripping down the walls of the Church. In the evening the fire gained new life, completely destroying another 11 storey tenement. At the end of it all blackened ruins lay everywhere. Two firemen and 11 citizens were dead and 400 families were homeless while the cost to the city was £200,000.

Despite harsh beginnings the new Fire Brigade survived. Braidwood and his men were dedicated to their work and the new firemen were often out training in the city streets at 4am. At this early hour they could practise without interruption and in dark conditions. Another of their routines was climbing up and down the North Bridge on long ropes doing rescue drills. The men wore blue jackets with brass buttons, hard leather helmets and white canvas trousers. They were the first municipal fire-brigade in Britain and one of the first in Europe. So from chaotic and dismal beginnings grew a fire-fighting profession with a great tradition of dedication and efficiency, a history for Edinburgh to be proud of.

The Heave Awa' Disaster

On the 25th day of November in 1861 at about 1.30am as most of the city slept there occurred a great disaster in the Old Town of Edinburgh. The *Edinburgh Evening Courant* reported it as 'One of the most appalling accidents that has ever taken place in the history of our city'. An 8-storey building described as 'an immense, tall and thickly populated tenement' suddenly collapsed. Of 77 residents more than 50 lay helpless under the rubble. Frantic efforts began almost immediately to pull the survivors to safety. The high building dated from around 1700 had at one time been home for those of 'rank and family' but in the 1800's had been 'given up to a great extent to the families of the labouring classes'.

William McLusky was a typical resident of the tenement. He was a shoemaker who lived on the 3rd floor with his wife and elderly mother. In the same household there lived Bridget McKinnon — their servant girl, Mrs Beveridge — a lodger, and finally 12 year old Joseph McIvor (Mr McLusky's nephew). In the cramped social conditions of the day it was not unusual to find so many living in one small apartment.

On the night of the disaster at about 8pm the McLuskys heard a loud crack. Mr McLusky investigated and checked all the walls and floorboards, but found nothing. His wife however was uneasy and worried about this unusual noise. The household was busy that night.

Shoemakers who did work for Mr McLusky were coming and going collecting their wages. Mrs McLusky voiced her fears to everyone who arrived. One of these men said later that she had even discussed with him and her husband what they would do if the building was to collapse. If only they had taken heed of her premonition.

The sound she had fretted over was probably one of the final signs of fatigue in the backbone of the building. A massive central wall had previously been weakened by the alterations to a ground-floor shop. In order to gain more storage space the owner had demolished sections of the wall, leaving only pillars to support the enormous weight. This great structure was further at risk as it was not actually attached to the gable ends of the tenement.

Cracks had been investigated in the basement by one of the shopkeepers on Saturday, but a thorough inspection had been put off until Monday, 24 hours too late to save any lives.

So the McLusky household retired to their beds and like so many others were too deep in sleep to hear the final sounds of 'yielding timbers' that some of those who managed to escape reported.

At approximately 1.30am the weary legs of the central wall finally buckled and collapsed. Every floor was pulled down with it and the McLuskys and 50 others lay under a blanket of tons of rubble and masonry.

Witnesses in the street raised the alarm immediately and as the dust started to clear the confused cries of the injured and dying began to rise from the remains of the building.

Soon magistrates, firemen and many volunteers were labouring in the bitter cold of the November night, searching for survivors. The torches of the rescuers swarmed and danced over the ruins. They quickly converged on any signs of life and cheers would go up as survivors were drawn from the rubble. Most were rescued in the first few hours but as time went on more and more corpses were uncovered. Of the McLusky household, Mrs Beveridge, the lodger, was the first to be found. She was taken out alive but later died of her injuries. The servant girl Bridget McKinnon was found dead.

Mr McLusky's nephew, Joseph McIvor, had been located early in the rescue operations, but the remains of the building refused to give him up. During the persistent efforts to reach him, his brave shouts were followed. He was 'heard to encourage those toiling on his behalf by calling out, 'heave awa' men I'm no dead yet''. Finally he was rescued from the rubble, a very plucky survivor. Eventually at 6 am Mr McLusky's 67 year old mother was rescued. She was the last to be found alive. After this only the dead lay waiting. There was no sign of Mr and Mrs McLusky.

As dawn began to break the full extent of the disaster became clear. The gable ends and the back wall still stood and the rubble now blocked the whole street. As the light grew it was possible to look up and see where each floor had been. Fire places set in the walls could still be seen burning away, kettles and coffee pots still on the hob. In other recesses were more signs of life, jars and biscuit tins left completely undisturbed. In one window there was even a bird cage, inside it a linnet song bird. It hopped to and fro in the cold November wind, too high up to be rescued.

It was late on Monday afternoon that the bodies of Mr and Mrs McLusky were found. Digging operations carried on for the rest of the week trying to locate the final victims. There was in fact one final rescue on the Tuesday morning. A fireman risked his life climbing a long ladder to reach the linnet song bird. After descending from the high window, cage in hand, the fireman received several offers to buy the hardy bird, but he refused them all and kept this last survivor in his own house for many years.

Eventually the authorities were able to confirm the final death toll. Thirty-five people had lost their lives in the disaster. No longer would citizens of the Old Town be able to purchase a pair of William McLusky's shoes.

It was on Tuesday the 26th of November 1861 that he and his wife made their final journey up the Royal Mile. Their bodies were being taken from the Canongate Police Station to be buried in the Greyfriars Churchyard. It is perhaps fitting that the procession paused for a moment opposite the ruins of 99-107 High Street. Onlookers went silent and workmen stopped digging as a mark of respect.

Of their household only their nephew, young Joseph McIvor had survived and when it came to commemorating the events they would have been proud to know that above what is now Paisley Close there is still a bust of Joseph. Around him are his famous words 'Heave awa' chaps, I'm no dead yet'.

Chapter Four

Witchcraft

B etween 1479 and 1722 more than 4000 men and women were burnt as witches in Scotland. Of that total over 300 were executed on the Castlehill in Edinburgh. During the reign of King James VI it is claimed that more witches were 'worryit' (strangled and then burnt) on the Castlehill than in any other part of the Kingdom.

But Scotland was not alone in its harsh treatment of witches, because there has always been a fear of witches throughout the world, and indeed throughout history. Although a scattering of witch beliefs has always been evident, it was in the 16th and 17th centuries that there was a tremendous increase in the European consciousness of witchcraft. Many believe this arose out of religious, political and economic conflicts of the age, encouraged by the churchmen of the Renaissance, Reformation and Counter-Reformation.

It was in 1640 that the Scottish General Assembly advised ministers 'carefully to take notice of witches, charmers and all such abuses of the people'.

Witchcraft had become recognised as the work of the Devil. Witches were believed to have consciously put themselves under the Devil's command while fulfilling their own depraved desires. This belief fostered the idea that the main way of identifying a witch was to determine whether he or she had made a pact with the Devil.

The accused witches were usually poor, eccentric or unpopular and were very rarely given a fair trial. The intimidating atmosphere and the assumption of guilt more often than not meant that the trial just became a breeding ground for further accusations. In Edinburgh's history many harsh methods were used by the witch hunters to expose those who were believed to be in league with the Devil.

Torture was highly recommended because unlike England, the Scottish authorities would accept a confession as evidence. If a supposed witch could be maimed into confessing a pact with the Devil he or she could be convicted. As the screws were tightened and the ropes strained and creaked, the unfortunate accused was now in a complete Catch 22. The presumption of guilt was so strong that if they did not confess freely it was assumed they were still under Satan's will. Excruciating pain would be inflicted until that will was broken.

One easy way to identify a witch was to find the 'Devil's Mark'. These marks were moles, scars, and other ordinary skin blemishes supposedly made by the Devil's teeth. They were said to be his way of branding a witch as one of his own. Everyone has these marks, so we might all have been executed if examined. But it would all have depended on the witch hunter or 'witch pricker'. They prodded the skin with sharp pins and if any of these blemishes seemed insensitive to pain or did not bleed then it could be assumed that it was a Devil's mark.

Of course all this required a great deal of experience, skill, and often quite a bit of cheating. Witch hunters were paid on a commission basis! One Scot was even asked to travel to Newcastle-on-Tyne in England where he was offered 20 shillings per witch and, not surprisingly, discovered 15.

The Nor'Loch was a body of water which lay approximately where Princes Street Gardens are today. It was formed in the 15th century and acted as part of the city's defences till the late 1700's. Its connection with witchcraft is best illustrated by the 'evidence' it gave in the trial of Elsie Peat in 1589.

This elderly lady who was rather eccentric, was often heard muttering away to herself as she went about her business in the Old Town of Edinburgh. Many locals were suspicious of her and superstitious gossip spread that her innocent mumblings were actually conversations with the Devil. She was accused of witchcraft and the Nor'Loch gave the old woman her trial. At this time it was believed that witches were lighter than normal people and it was this belief that carried her down to the edge of the loch, her thumbs tied securely to her toes. Trussed up like this, she was thrown in. If she sank down into the murky waters and drowned she would be termed innocent and given a Christian burial, if she floated she would be found guilty. Her chances of survival were slim. It is believed that air pockets in her clothing caused her to bob to the surface. Her guilt confirmed, she was carried back up the steep hill and strangled and burned like so many others, in front of Edinburgh Castle.

A Royal Witch Trial

King James VI of Scotland was personally involved in a witch trial which took place in 1590/91. The 'North Berwick Witches' story is one of sorcery, treason and politics and remains to this day the most famous of all Scottish cases. It is also a fascinating illustration of simple accusations developing into quite spectacular claims.

It all started when the Deputy Bailie of Tranent, David Seaton, accused his maid-servant of witchcraft. He tortured her with the 'pilliwinks' - a harmless enough name for what were in fact the exruciatingly painful thumbscrews. After a Devil's mark was found on her she was subjected to more torture. She finally confessed to being in league with the Devil and also implicated many others.

Four of those named were brought to trial — Dr John Fian (a schoolmaster), Euphemia Maclean (daughter of a Lord), Barbara Napier and Agnes Sampson (a midwife).

To the King and the witch hunters John Fian was considered the most prominent figure in the North Berwick coven. After some horrific tortures he confessed to being 'clerk to all those that were in subjection to the Devil's service'. He also mentioned Francis Hepburn, Earl of Bothwell — a man who had a claim to the throne should the King die without heirs. Bothwell was also known to be interested in the occult.

After his ordeal, John Fian was put in prison where he recovered enough to escape a few days later. When re-captured, he again proclaimed his innocence. Despite renewed torture, he refused to confess. His strong resistance was assumed to be due to his meeting the Devil during his escape. He was sent to the Castlehill on

January 31st 1591 and there he was burnt, affirming his innocence to the end.

Agnes Sampson was the complete opposite. After torture, the tales of witchcraft gushed forth. It was she who made the startling claim that she and the others had conspired on more than one occasion to kill the King. According to Agnes, on All Hallow's Eve over 200 witches met to try and sink the King's ship on his return from Denmark. The sorcery involved a cat, venom of toad and the joints of a dead man. She too talked of Bothwell, except in more detail. She described how at one meeting they passed round a wax image of the King saying 'This is King James VI ordained to be consumed at the instance of a noble man, Francis Earl of Bothwell'. Were these simply Agnes's imaginary ravings, or the careful prompting of the King's advisers?

After torture Euphemia Maclean and Barbara Napier confirmed many of these details and no doubt added a few of their own.

At one point the tales were becoming so far-fetched that the King declared that the witches were 'all extreme liars'. Then came the final twist in the story. Agnes Sampson went up to the King and whispered something in his ear about his wedding night.

The King declared that 'all the Devils in Hell' could not have known of what she said. Nobody knows what she said or why, because it certainly sealed her fate, and the King was forced to accept their stories.

Agnes Sampson and Euphemia Maclean were burnt on the Castlehill. Barbara Napier was also condemned but was eventually released. When Bothwell escaped to Italy, never to return, this famous case finally petered out and no-one else was brought to trial.

The King went on to write a book called 'Daemonology' in 1597. It is believed that the King's book was very popular in North Berwick.

Reading through the witchcraft cases recorded in Edinburgh is a fascinating exercise, for example:

Bessie Dunlop — Tried in 1576 for witchcraft. One of the crimes was several meetings with a man called Tam Reid. This may not seem incredible, but it should be noted that Tam died at the Battle of Pinkie 29 years beforehand.

Isabel Young — 'Worryit at a stake' for making various people ill in 1600.

James Reid — In 1608 he claimed to have met the Devil and also tried to destroy the crops of David Liberton by putting a piece of enchanted flesh under his mill door. He was taken from the court straight to the Castlehill to be ... well, you know the routine.

5 Witches — Mareon Angus, Heline Herioat, Bessy Lacoast, Allisoune Fermor and Jean Sydserfe were all strangled and burnt together in March 9th 1659 because they had 'danced with the Devil'.

Agnes Fynnie — An unfortunate lady who was almost certainly only guilty of being 'crabbit' with her neighbours. She stayed in Lord Cullen's Close and managed to scrape a living as a small dealer in groceries. Well-known for her temper and sharp tongue, she probably made a few enemies. There were four main charges. It was claimed that she made Isabel Atchesone fall off a horse and break her leg, made Margaret Williamson blind by the use of sorcery, and drove Andrew Wilson mad. Perhaps the most serious charge was her threat to persuade the Devil to come and bite Bettie Currie (she probably deserved it). Agnes Fynnie confessed in front of the Court of Session and said she had been a witch for 28 years. Sentenced to death, she was burnt at the stake in 1641.

Lady Jane Douglas

If the image of a witch is someone who is poor, ugly and old, Lady Jane Douglas was precisely the opposite. She was young, rich and 'the most renowned beauty in Britain' when accused of witchcraft.

This case also involved a Scottish king, except this time there is a hint of revenge to accompany the smell of politics.

It was in the reign of King James V that Lord Glamis died leaving the beautiful Lady Jane as a very desirable widow. Her keenest suitor was a man called William Lyon who had asked her to marry him on a number of occasions. Lady Jane decided that he wasn't the man for her and she actually married Archibald Campbell of Skipness. It is said that Lyon vowed to have his revenge.

She was later to be accused of attempting to kill the king with poison and sorcery. Even at the time many considered the charges absurd. Lady Jane was arrested along with her husband, son and elderly priest and all four were incarcerated in Edinburgh Castle. She was most likely being used as a political short cut to eliminate her husband who may have been a threat to the King.

The accuser of Lady Jane? He was, of course, the one and only William Lyon, the rebuffed suitor.

After horrific tortures, Lady Jane confessed to her 'crimes' and was sentenced to death. On 17th July 1537 she was led out through the castle gates to the execution site on the Castlehill. 'Barrels tarred and faggots (wood) oiled, were piled around her and she was burned to ashes within view of her son and husband, who beheld the terrible scene from the tower that overlooked it'.

The next night poor Archibald Campbell tried to escape from the castle but slipped and fell to his death on the rocks below. Lady Jane's son was held in the castle for five years before being released.

There are differing opinions as to how much the King knew and how involved he was in the accusations. Some say he knew nothing and was so struck with remorse that he had the family's old priest released and William Lyon banished from the Kingdom; a light sentence for the lying Lyon who had instigated such pain and misery on Lady Jane Douglas and her family.

The Wizard of the West Bow

The most famous case of witchcraft in the Old Town is that of Major Thomas Weir, a man whose trial meant the fall from being one of the most respected members of Edinburgh society to a shameful death by strangulation and burning.

Thomas Weir was born at the very end of the 16th Century in 1599, near the town of Carluke in Strathclyde. He joined the army as a young officer and eventually rose to the rank of Major in the Earl of Lanark's regiment. At the age of 50, having left the army, he took up the post of Captain of the City Guard.

After a long and impeccable career in uniform he finally retired to civilian life. It was at this time that he moved from the Cowgate to the West Bow and began to devote himself whole-heartedly to his religion. He became part of a then well known sect, known locally as the 'Bowhead Saints' because of their strict religious beliefs. This sect met in each other's houses, had religious discussions and led fervent prayers for several hours a day.

Major Weir was well known in the Old Town area and was described as a tall dark figure with a large nose and grim features. He was usually clad in a black cloak and was rarely seen without his trusty walking stick. His imposing figure combined well with his excellent preaching. Major Weir possessed a graceful, sighing voice, which made him very popular with those who came to listen to his sermons. He was so admired and respected by his fellow 'Saints' that slowly he became their unofficial leader and earned himself the nickname 'Angelical Thomas'.

Over the years his reputation spread beyond the city walls and guests of all ranks felt honoured if they were able to attend one of his prayer meetings, even if it was only to listen from an adjacent room.

In the spring of 1670, Major Weir hosted what was to be his final prayer meeting. As usual a great crowd began to gather from near and far at Major Weir's home in the West Bow. The whole house was filled with a low murmur as everyone awaited the entrance of the great preacher. As he entered the whispering died away, he took up his position and prepared to speak.

Although now 70 years of age and failing in health, his reputation was as strong as ever. He could quote long passages of the Bible from memory and enthral a meeting with his hypnotic voice. This man was a pillar of society, a man whose nickname came from being more 'angel' than mortal. Nobody could have anticipated what was to happen that night.

The sermon started normally and no-one suspected anything was wrong until he began to falter. It was to the absolute shock and horror of all present when he began to confess to leading a double life. On the one hand a 'Bowhead Saint', respected by all, on the other, someone who had committed great acts of bestiality, including incest. Even more shocking to this highly religious gathering were his claims that he made a pact with the Devil and had met him on a number of occasions.

Major Weir was ushered from the room by his friends and the stunned audience began to disperse, many in tears.

He was kept out of the public eye after this and the news was put out that he was ill. Day after day his friends tried to persuade him to renounce his confessions, but he was adamant and would not be swayed.

In such a close community it was not possible to keep anything hushed up for long. A minister called John Sinclair, who had been at the meeting, reported the extraordinary events to the authorities. They decided to investigate and sent doctors to examine Weir. He was found to be of sound body and mind, still refusing to repent. This was to lead to his trial in April 1670.

Local residents were now coming forward and all sorts of previous suspicions were being confirmed and used as evidence. Even Major Weir's staff was taken into custody as it was said to have magical properties.

Major Weir was found guilty of 'carnal offences' and on the 14th of April was taken outside the city to a place called the Gallow Lee. It was in front of a large noisy crowd that his death sentence was carried out. Thousands watched as the 'Wizard of the West Bow' was strangled and then burnt. His last words were 'I have lived as a beast, I shall die as a beast'. Even his walking stick provided a spectacle as it reputedly twisted and turned like a serpent in the flames.

This is not the end of the story, if the locals were to be believed. As far as they were concerned, Major Weir may have perished, but his spirit was still with them in the old town. Across the narrow alleyways the stories of strange sightings and appearances rebounded from doorway to doorway, gathering details, evolving from hearsay into fact.

People crossed the street when they passed his house, and those who dared to glance through the windows saw objects flying around the rooms. Someone had even seen a coach drawn by six headless horses careering down the West Bow. Inside, some said, could be seen Major Weir, his eyes burning red, his face gaunt and skeletal, off to meet his friend the Devil. Not all made such extravagant claims. Some simply said that they had heard Major Weir's distinctive sigh as they passed his old house.

At the time these were not stories, but facts that convinced locals that Major Weir's house was uninhabitable.

The superstitions must have been very strong because the building lay empty from 1670 to 1820 — one and a half centuries. In 1820 a family called Patullo moved in encouraged by a low rent and apparently unconcerned with the tales about the building. There were raised eyebrows and curious glances as the new furniture crossed the threshold. The Patullos claimed that not long after they had moved in, objects began to move around the rooms. One night a calf's head appeared above the end of the bed. It was all too much and they left, never to return.

With this new confirmation of all the old fears, the building again lay empty till finally in the 1870's the whole block was demolished.

Although the structure is gone you can still go down the West Bow and listen as you pass for the graceful sigh of the preacher turned wizard — Major Weir.

The Ordeal of Touch

So the witch hunters searched for those who were in league with the Devil and used his powers to further his domain. It is obvious from witch-pricking and ducking that very superstitious beliefs were used to ascertain guilt. There were some cases which did not involve witchcraft but used similar superstitions, only this time it was in the name of God.

It was believed that if a suspected murderer was to touch the victim and blood was to flow from the mouth, nostrils or wound of the dead person, then the suspect was assumed guilty.

Sir James Stanfield was a wealthy merchant of Edinburgh in the 1600's. He had a town house in World's End Close in the Royal Mile, very near to a bar which still bears the name Stanfield's. It was in November 1687 that he was found dead, face down in a pool of water on his estate near Edinburgh. Everyone assumed he had died of natural causes until it was discovered that Sir James's wife had purchased mourning clothes a few days before his death.

Naturally the authorities were slightly suspicious. Doctors were called to examine the body and they claimed there were signs of strangulation.

Philip Stanfield was suspected of being his father's murderer and he was forced to carry out the 'ordeal of touch'. Sir James's body did bleed after being touched by his son and this was considered weighty evidence. The family servants were tortured until their confessions added to the pressure for a verdict of guilty. So it was that on the 15th of February 1688 Philip Stanfield was hanged for murder.

Sir George Mackenzie, one of the public prosecutors at the trial, commented on the results of Philip Stanfield's 'ordeal of touch' to the jury. He said 'God Almighty Himself was pleased to bear a share in the testimonies which we produce'. Superstition had won.

The last words came from James Miller who wrote a poem about the event:

'Young Stanfield touched his father's corpse
When rose a fearful wail
For blood gushed out the winding sheet
And every face grew pale'.

Even after the last witch trials in Scotland the superstitious beliefs did not necessarily disappear.

On the south-eastern side of the city is the Holyrood Park. Arthur's Seat is the volcanic hill which rises to 823 feet above sea-level. It was in 1836 that a very strange discovery was made on the north-eastern slope — seventeen small coffins each about six inches in length. Inside every coffin was a tiny 'corpse' in its own clothing. Many at the time associated the discovery with witchcraft. The coffins can still be seen in Royal Museum of Scotland in Chambers Street in Edinburgh.

The Castlehill was where most of the burning of witches took place and this fact has been commemorated by John Duncan's bronze plaque made in 1894. Although there is no water coming out, this plaque is actually meant to be a drinking fountain and is attached to the westward wall of the Castlehill reservoir (facing the esplanade). It shows the two sides of witchcraft. On the left hand side the evil witch is depicted while on the other side is the witch who uses her powers for good. The water tray beneath has the 'evil eye' on the left and the 'healing hands' on the right.

To get the atmosphere of this spot you should wander up to the very top of the Royal Mile on a dark moonless night and gaze across the Esplanade to the Castle. Try to imagine the scenes as crowds gathered to witness the burning of yet another witch in the Old Town of Edinburgh. Sometimes the wind howls across this exposed area and it is easy to imagine the sound being the wail of tortured souls, innocent victims of witchcraft. If you feel a shiver down your spine it's hardly surprising!

Chapter Five

Ghosts and the Supernatural

'I love to tread this ancient way
when evening gilds the sky
And tiny window lights appear
on buildings gaunt and high'

(Nan McDonald 1944)

Anyone who has stood in a dark narrow close between 'buildings gaunt and high' in the Old Town of Edinburgh can imagine why so many ghost stories abound in the city. A fearful soul standing in these murky chasms would find that on a wild moonless night the shadows can easily deceive and the echoes confuse.

This atmosphere combined with a genuine fear of the Devil and the powers of darkness gave rise to many an uncanny tale. These stories were swapped in the taverns of Auld Reekie, stretching the imaginations of the most bleary eyed listeners and sobering them up into rapt attention. As they stumbled home, the drinkers would be watching the shadows, dreading an encounter with Old Horny, Satan, Nick or Clootie. All the different names for the Devil, their fear of whom was often fostered by the fiery sermons of their ministers each Sunday.

The following tales describe some of the strange and unnatural occurrences recorded throughout the centuries in Edinburgh's Old Town.

The Ghostly Herald

Perhaps the city's oldest ghost story concerns the market cross, the place from which many important City and Royal proclamations were made. It was here that the Coronation of Queen Elizabeth was announced in 1954. More than 400 years earlier, another famous announcement was made from the Cross. In this case it was announcement before the event. A prediction of disaster.

On a warm August evening in 1513, Richard Lawson, a local merchant, was taking the air on the first floor gallery of his house when he saw a ghostly herald appear at the Cross. This herald proceeded to announce the names of men who were soon to meet violent and bloody deaths.

The list began with King James IV, followed by the names of the cream of Scotland's nobility. Finally Richard Lawson's name was also called. Until that moment, he had stood transfixed, but on hearing his name he fell to his knees and prayed fervently for his life.

Richard Lawson must have been a brave man because at the beginning of September he was one of thousands of men who marched south following his King despite the awful prediction. In 1512 King Henry VIII had attacked France. The French had persuaded the Scots to invade England from the north. James IV had assembled one of the largest and best equipped armies in Scottish history — at least 35,000 men. The English army was led by the Earl of Surrey and they clashed on the 9th of September 1513 at Flodden Field. The Scots were massacred. The King was hacked to pieces along with 15 lowland earls, 70 barons and hundreds of knights. Ten thousand perished, some families almost ceased to exist. Edinburgh's Lord Provost, Sir Alexander Lauder was slain alongside many of the city's brave citizens.

Of the list read by the herald only Richard Lawson survived and he told the story to Lindsay of Pitscottie, a Scottish historian not averse to the odd ghost story. His account of Richard Lawson's experiences has stayed with us for 400 years. The ghostly herald has never been seen again.

The Laughing Lady

Sometimes tales of strange occurrences came after the trials of supposed witches. The 'evidence' that arose at the trial would become more and more far-fetched as locals retold their stories to justify the suspicions, 'they'd always had' about the activities of the supposed witch. Perhaps the best example of these superstitious outbursts comes from the case of Major Thomas Weir.

After he had been burnt various stories grew up around him. It was common knowledge at one time that everyone in the West Bow area knew someone, who knew someone, whose wife's brother had had a terrifying experience near Major Weir's house. One such story was told by a woman and her servant who were walking up the Bow late one night. As they neared Major Weir's house a gigantic female figure leapt up in front of them. This huge apparition was shaking with uncontrollable laughter as it started to move slowly down the West Bow. The woman and her servant followed it till it turned into an alleyway called Stinking Close. The Close was filled with torches and unholy merriment. No theory has ever been ventured to explain the apparition's good humour.

The Headless Drummer

Edinburgh Castle is haunted by the spectre of a headless drummer. This story probably originates from a tale of 1650 when a soldier on sentry duty heard the slow beat of a drum on the Esplanade. He challenged the figure and on hearing no answer fired his musket. When the alarm was raised nothing was found and the sentry was replaced. The same thing happened again. Even the Governor himself, Colonel Walter Dundas heard the clanking of armour and the tramp of feet. This was believed to be a warning to the soldiers in the castle of impending war. This prediction proved accurate. After defeating a Scottish army at Dunbar, Cromwell's forces entered Edinburgh in September 1650. They surrounded the castle and on Christmas Eve, after three long months of seige, Colonel Dundas and his men surrendered.

The Flescher's Wife

This cautionary tale comes from the end of the 17th Century and concerns an Edinburgh 'flescher' or butcher. His wife had died leaving him with four very young children. Just 3 days after the burial of his wife he was off to 'console' himself with a lady friend who resided in Provost's Close. During the evening the romance was considerably dampened by the appearance at the window of the gray, cold face

of the butcher's wife wrapped in trailing grave clothes. The butcher fled the house but a few days later he braved a return and again the apparition appeared at the window. This proved to be too much for him and he fell into a mysterious sickness. He never recovered and soon departed from this world to make his excuses 'in some other place'.

Lady Primrose and the Magic Mirror

Lady Eleanor Campbell was born into Edinburgh's high society and it was while she was still a teenager that she became the wife of the powerful James Viscount Primrose.

Apparently her husband's character was not as sweet as his name. One night he made an attempt on her life and she only narrowly escaped injury. As Lady Primrose ran screaming from the house her husband fled in the opposite direction. He was not seen again and it was believed that he had gone abroad.

A few years later Lady Primrose went with some friends to see a travelling Italian sorcerer in the Canongate. He was said to have strange powers and also possessed a magical mirror. Being curious as to the whereabouts of her husband, Lady Primrose asked the sorcerer if he could enlighten her. Apparently she was shown to the magical mirror and told to observe closely what she could see.

At first she could see nothing but then images began to form themselves into a hazy picture. It seemed to be a Church scene. In the centre a couple were being married. As she peered closer she realised to her amazement that the man about to be married was her husband. While she was still trying to recover from this, another figure came on the scene. This person was gesticulating wildly and could then be seen drawing his sword. Although she could not be sure, Lady Primrose felt that the third character had all the mannerisms of her brother and he too was known to be abroad at that time.

Before the action could continue the magical mirror clouded over.

Still stunned by all this, Lady Primrose decided to take an exact note of what she had seen and at what time it had occurred. When her brother returned she immediately went to tell him her story. He said that he was indeed the third figure in the scene she described. By pure coincidence he had been invited by a Dutch merchant and his wife to their daughter's wedding. Lady Primrose's brother was delighted to attend, especially since their daughter was marrying a fellow Scotsman. Imagine his surprise when he saw his own brother-in-law at the altar. He managed to prevent the wedding but the whole incident could not have been beneficial to Scottish/Dutch relations.

Lady Primrose compared her own notes on the various events and lo and behold both accounts were exactly the same even to the hour at which they occurred.

This charming little story is used as a basis for what is considered to be one of Sir Walter Scott's best short stories 'My Aunt Margaret's Mirror'.

Lord Primrose was to die in 1706. Lady Primrose was remarried within two years to the 2nd Earl of Stair. It was on the 27th of March 1708 that she became Lady Stair and was said to be much happier in her second marriage.

Named after her, Lady Stair's House still stands in a quiet courtyard behind the Lawnmarket. It is now a city museum exhibiting relics of Robert Burns, Sir Walter Scott and Robert Louis Stevenson. No magical mirrors are on display as far as we know, but the building should perhaps be known as Lady Campbell Primrose Stair's House to remind us all of this magical story.

Town Guard Ghost

The Old Town is still haunted by one of its now extinct town guard. In 1818 Sir Walter Scott described the 'spectre' of an old grey-headed and grey-bearded Highland Town Guard who still carries his Lochaber axe round the statue of King Charles II in

Parliament Square. So if you catch a glimpse of a muddy red uniform, or should a withered hand fall on your shoulder, don't scream, it's only the very long arm of the law, stretching out through time.

Angus Roy

In 1820 a sailor from Leith was forced to return to the Old Town of Edinburgh. He had been forced to leave his sea-faring life because of an accident. He had fallen from a high mast and although he survived, he remained crippled for the rest of his life. He was not fond of being a 'land-lubber' and longed for the sea. To make matters worse, the last 20 years of his life were made a misery by many of the local children. They teased and tormented him, ran behind him mocking the strange drag and hop walk he had acquired after the accident. Never happy, he finally died in 1840 in the Victoria Terrace area.

It was claimed that he had vowed to take his revenge on the people of the area who had caused him so much misery. Even to this day he is sometimes seen dragging his leg along Victoria Terrace. Poor Angus Roy, the sad and tormented sailor.

The Woman in Black Silk

James Bone in his book '*Edinburgh Revisited*' describes a ghost of the late 1800's to be found in Chessel's Court in the Canongate. The story was told to him by a lady of the Gordon family. She lived in the top flat and her story was corroborated by another old lady in the same stair. It was a well-known story of the Court that a woman had 'hanged hersel. . .' 'or something' in the building. Although this particular woman had never actually seen the ghost, she had been 'near seeing it'. Quite often heavy breathing could be heard outside the door, but if she went to investigate, there was nothing to be found. She did say that her brother had seen the ghost one night when he was staying with her. She said he saw 'a tall woman in black silk, the dress stuck oot a' roond and near took up the hale room. He couldna see the face o' it, for it was awfu' tall, just as the folk said'.

Her brother refused to stay with her after this but the story of the strange woman in black silk was now confirmed for all in the building.

The Ghost in the Mortuary

It wasn't long ago that the basement of the present-day High Street Police Station was used as a mortuary. One of the distinctive characters who worked there was a man well-known for his hefty, lumbering build, bald head and 'sticky-oot' ears. It was said that when he wore his huge white apron at work he looked more like a baker than a mortuary attendant.

One of his eccentricities was American Comics. Popeye stories were amongst his favourites and he was rarely seen without a comic about his person. He must have loved his work because even though he was assigned an office he shunned it for the peaceful atmosphere in the mortuary itself. He would prefer to sit amongst his charges, tea in one hand, comic in the other.

After many years of devoted service he was found dead one night. Even in death he could not be parted from his beloved workplace. It was not long afterwards that the first reports came in of a strange white figure that appeared at night in the mortuary. Whether or not this figure was carrying a cup of tea and a comic has never been revealed.

The Witchery Chair

When fantastic stories of shimmering apparitions are told they are sometimes hard to believe. But not long ago, in November 1986, a mortal acquaintance of mine was sitting in the Witchery Restaurant late one evening. Only the staff remained. Suddenly, the silence was broken by the sound of a chair scraping across the stone floor. When the young man looked up, he saw a chair move 6 to 10 inches back from a table as if someone was getting up. This was a simple occurence, but as the young man said ' When it happens to you and you can see absolutely no possible explanation, it is a very unnerving experience.'

The Onyx Ring

In 1978 a young Edinburgh man was walking past an antique shop in Broughton Street when he spied out of the corner of his eye a gold ring with a black onyx stone. He was quite taken by it and upon closer examination found that the second-hand ring had a man's face on it. The salesman was unable to tell him anything about it.

During the winter of 1980-81 this same man was renovating an old building in the High Street when the ring fell from his finger into the rubble. Despite a thorough search he could find nothing, so he forgot about it as he and his partner were on a tight schedule, busy cleaning up the mess in order to open their new shop on time.

One morning 6 months later, after the shop had been opened,

a member of the staff found the ring, clean, bright and undamaged lying in the middle of the now carpeted floor.

Although confused as to how it had suddenly reappeared, the shop owner was delighted to have his ring back. But his joy was short lived. Not long afterwards when working in another area of the shop, still being converted, he lost his ring again. This time members of staff were present and all helped in the search but nothing was found.

Two months later in the staff-room a lady dropped her own ring down the side of a settee and when she reached down to get it, she pulled out 2 rings. The black onyx had re-appeared.

Unfortunately, there is no neat ending to this mystery. In 1983 the ring disappeared again but this time the shop-owner did not search for it and being superstitious claims he does not want to find it.

Was it all just coincidence? Whose was the face on the ring? Will it ever re-appear? Perhaps we will never know.

The Mysterious Mary King's Close

All through Edinburgh's history, buildings have risen and fallen along the steep ridge known as the Royal Mile. Of all the places in the Old Town of Edinburgh that excite the curiosity of adult and child alike, there can be no example to compare with Mary King's Close.

The name of this alleyway probably comes from a lady who at one time owned many properties in the area. It was a typical, bustling warren of life until it was struck by fire in 1750. Four years later the empty site became home for the new Royal Exchange which in turn in 1811 became the City Chambers of Edinburgh. Despite all the changes, 65 feet of Mary King's Close still lies submerged deep under the present buildings.

The idea of a 'hidden close' being under the city is one reason why it arouses such curiosity. The other is the darker side of its history.

The first suggestion that some of its occupants were not of this world seems to some from a book called '*Satan's Invisible World Displayed*', published in 1685. One of the tales centres on the experiences of Thomas Coltheart and his wife. Shortly after moving into Mary King's Close they were confronted by the apparition of a human head with grey beard, suspended in mid air.

They also saw the phantom of a child, plus dogs, cats and other 'strange unearthly beings' floating around their rooms.

The moral of the story seems to be in the way that the Colthearts dealt with these terrible apparitions. Each night they fell to their knees and prayed. Shortly thereafter the same apparitions disappeared, never to return. Many years after the Colthearts had moved away the new occupants, an old soldier and his wife, reported the same type of things. They did not stay to brave the unknown and left immediately, presumably not having prayed hard enough.

Since then other stories have been connected with Mary King's Close. Sometimes scratching can be heard through the walls. This is claimed to be a chimney sweep who died while trapped inside the chimney. Another concerns one of the rooms adjoining the close which is often strangely cold. Who knows? Perhaps it is the old room of the Colthearts.

Although it is never advertised, there is a constant flow of enquiries from all types of groups to the City Chambers asking for access. (There's a long waiting list). The surprising interest in Mary King's Close has come from the exaggerated rumour in Edinburgh of a city beneath the city, stories of how you can walk the old streets and see the old shop windows, mouldy bread still lying there etc. These vivid stories combined with the tales of hauntings of the past, catch the attention of so many of Edinburgh's present day citizens that Mary King's Close is guaranteed a mysterious aura for many years to come.

Compared with the experiences of the Colthearts, the ghostly activity in Mary King's Close seems to have greatly decreased. Despite this, there are those who claim 'strange unearthly beings' still inhabit the City Chambers to this day.

These last stories show that Edinburgh, as always, will continue to be a place full of secrets. It is exciting to think that between the walls and under the stones lie yet more clues to the discovery and understanding of the places and the people that have given the Old Town such a fascinating and mysterious history.